CW01432529

Why Me?

Why It's Not Just About The Money

Belinda Mangani

WHY ME?
Why It's Not Just About The Money

For general information on our other products and services, please find our contact information online at www.belindamangani.com.

DEDICATION

In loving memory of my beautiful friend Katia, who sadly lost her battle to breast cancer far too early in life.

To my beautiful family,

Thank you for providing me with not just daily inspiration and motivation, but challenging me to always be better in everything I do.

May you continue to grow and prosper in everything you do throughout this journey called life, knowing that in everything you do, I will always be there to love, guide and support you.

Because of you, I am truly excited for the day when I can visit your new homes, use a different glass for every sip I take, put purple nail polish on in the back of your nice new cars (accidentally leaving remnants on your nice new leather seats, of course) and turning on every light in every room— and then politely leaving the room.

Dad and I are excited for the day when we can finally park our shiny new mobile home in your driveway and hook up to your power.

For all this, I love you all unconditionally.

WHAT PEOPLE ARE SAYING ABOUT THE FIND YOUR ZERO WORKSHOPS

"Jacqui and I went through Belinda's 'Find your Zero' program and finally the penny dropped. You can't spend more than you earn! This sounds so simple but when you are not really in control of how you spend and you can't work out why you're not getting ahead, it's because money is controlling you. Belinda's simple step-by-step program digs deep into the real situation with your money and puts you back into control.

We all have dreams about what we want to do in life. Belinda's 'Find Your Zero' program is the place to start to turn dreams into a reality."

— Paul Thomson, Head of Social Responsibility

"I have had the pleasure of having Belinda work alongside my husband and I, and help us to create a future that is full of hope and promise. Belinda's enthusiasm and passion is infectious, her mentorship is invaluable and she has kept us accountable for the changes she has recommended. I feel very fortunate that our paths crossed, and now have a tremendous feeling of excitement about what kind of future we can create for our family."

— Sarah, Newport

"Six years ago, I was looking to buy my first home, but I had a seriously maxed-out credit card, an inherited debt from a failed marriage, and regardless of the money I was earning I could not manage to save anything.

A friend recommended that I give Belinda a call and I have never looked back! Belinda taught me how to manage my credit card and finances, and her knowledge of the mortgage products that would best suit me and my needs and meant that I was able to get my first mortgage within three months, without needing a guarantor or needing to give up the things I loved! I was over the moon.

Life changes, as it always does, and I have just started a family with my partner. We would like our family to grow, and to bring our children up on a property in the country, which means upsizing, however we are currently living on just my partners wage as our son is still just a baby. My first thought was to contact Belinda to see how we could make our dream a reality. Within two days, Belinda had us further reducing our debt by refinancing and consolidating our mortgages (my partner also has property and a personal loan) which is saving us hundreds of dollars a month! We are also working on further ways to reduce our debt to put us in a better position to make our dreams a reality and move into our own property in the country.

Belinda has an exceptional understanding of the products and services out there in the banking world, and has the brilliant skill of explaining it all, in a way that I could easily understand and remember—no jargon and nothing gets lost in translation! I have recommended her to friends in the past and will continue to do so in the future. Thank you, Belinda—you have changed my life for the better."

— **Claire & Sean, Upper Ferntree Gully**

"I cannot express how much Belinda has helped me understand the importance of managing money correctly. Her knowledge has helped me purchase my first home. Belinda takes pride in her work and also forms a relationship with her clients, to get to know their needs and makes recommendations suitable to each individual client. Her ongoing support has meant the world to me. It can feel daunting at times to understand the best way to manage your finances but with Belinda's help, I feel at ease. Please share this page with your family and friends and spread the word on the great work Belinda does. Thank you so much Belinda. I am forever grateful for your advice! She is truly a gem."

— **Rebecca, Essendon**

"I would have lost my house if it had not been for Belinda! I look back now (five years later) and I am amazed how Belinda saved me from financial disaster. I was in an almost-impossible predicament. Nowadays, I have a mortgage the size of the average car loan. I can't recommend Belinda highly enough!"

— **Sue, Williamstown**

"We would like to say a huge thank for all the help and guidance you have given us throughout the time we have known you. When we first met you, we were going through a difficult time and struggling financially.

We had always thought that everything was under control and that we knew exactly what we were doing, but we were wrong. You showed us how to use the money we had in a sensible manner that wouldn't leave us struggling more than we were.

With your extensive knowledge it has enabled us to know exactly how to better manager our finances. You gave me the courage and strength i needed to make the right and smart decisions.

Not only have you helped us, but through your knowledge we have also helped our children with their finances and taught them how to better manage their money.

From the bottom of our hearts Belinda, we would like to say thank you so much. We are so grateful that you have helped us in so many ways. I know your books will do the same for so many other people".

— **Leah and Martin**

"I wanted to send you a note to thank you for helping Frank and I change the course of our life.

After our initial consultation, I knew immediately that you were the right person for us. We have worked with other brokers before who to their credit are very knowledgeable but what separates you from the rest is WHY you do what you do; you GENUINELY want to help people succeed.

Doing the course helped us to realise that we were continuously making poor choices in our spending habits but it also brought to light that Frank and I share the same values and goals. We both wanted to make changes but just didn't know how to go about it.

You gave us hope when we thought there was no hope left.

— **Maria Cindric**

FIND OUT HOW YOU CAN JOIN OUR WORKSHOPS AT

www.belindamangani.com

Why you shouldn't wait for an emergency to occur before hitting the panic button.

Take action—reform and transform your life and money today.

Does your life feel like you are in a slow sinking boat, stuck trying to hold back the flood waters, or you simply took a wrong turn and got lost? Whatever it is for you, there are real solutions and guess what—they are simple and easy to follow.

Top 10 mistakes people make with their money and life

1. No life or money plan.
2. Only allocating minimum repayments to debts.
3. Never accumulating a safety net of surplus money.
4. Spending to mask life's real issues or disappointments.
5. Not connecting money management to better health and wellbeing.
6. Not taking control or responsibility for debt(s) until it's too late.
7. Surrounding or associating yourself with toxic people.
8. Constantly settling for second best in life.
9. Don't know how to fall down and get back up, with focus and determination.
10. Don't set achievable goals, which only leads to more disappointment.

Consider your answers to these few basic questions before we get started:

1. Are you sick of constantly working hard, earning good money, yet never seemingly making financial progress?
2. Are your debts and/or mortgage balance keeping you awake at night?
3. You love where you live, but really can't afford the affect the mortgage is having on your health and your relationships with your loved ones?
4. Is the ongoing stress and pressure of keeping up stopping you from enjoying the simple things in life?
5. Would you like a holiday without adding it to the credit card or feeling guilty?
6. Maybe you would prefer to have the freedom to make choices or the money to make positive decisions?
7. Are you feeling depressed, anxious or disappointed with your life?
8. Is fear of failure preventing you from moving forward?
9. Would you like to feel excited about what your future could look like?
10. Are you committed to doing whatever it takes?

ISN'T IT TIME YOU MADE THE CHANGE?

Guess what? If you answered yes, I think it's time! You are ready to embark on a journey to financial success. So, don't waste any more time—let's get started.

Remember though, this is not for the faint-hearted, or for those of you that want a quick fix. This journey will be one of excitement and fulfilment and I need to know that you are all buckled in and ready to take a leap of faith to improve not just your finances, but your life as well, forever.

TABLE OF CONTENTS

CHAPTER

1

Introduction

"There are people who have money and people who are rich."

— COCO CHANEL

For as long as I can remember, I have informally taught the principles of successful money management based on simple, easy-to-follow money strategies that I had learnt from a very young age and had successfully implemented with my own money. However, it wasn't until 2014 when I realised that, despite losing everything financially and starting over, that I was clearly doing something very different to most of my clients.

Having been asked to revisit them, I quickly discovered that they were all still pretty much at the same dollar amount financially as when I had met them ten years earlier. Actually, most even owed more than they did ten years earlier, yet had very little extra, or worse still *nothing* more to show for their increased debts. This led me to question myself: "How was it that we had gone to almost zero and back to $2 million-plus in ten years, actually superseding our original net worth, despite earning far less than all of them?"

I recognised that it was far from merely a fluke that we had achieved, but rather a secret, vital component that we had successfully implemented into our lives.

In answering this very question, I recognised that it was far from merely a fluke that we had achieved, but rather a secret, vital component that we had success-fully implemented into our lives. I identified that these very skills could also greatly enhance the outcomes of others, which lead me to introduce them formally to all my teachings in my Find Your Zero™ programs. So, why did I miss it, when it was right in front of me all that time? Simply because I had taken it for granted all my life, choosing to believe I was just better with money because I had been taught to save from a young age? I wish I could say it was that straightforward—today, I will share those principles with you.

For as long as I can remember I have always been one to dissect and analyse my life events and traumas in an attempt to constantly overcome and improve my own quality of life and I have imple-mented these very principles to my own money management throughout my life's journey. This is what I believe has contributed to me being able to climb back up from zero. The magic was in this powerful combination, and that led me to realise why my husband and I are doing something different to most. I have spent the past few years documenting, refining and concentrating on formulating and introducing this into my programs.

It's funny how life seems to constantly inject little spurts of wisdom and I often feel as though I am completing a massive puzzle, slowly slotting in the final pieces to build a masterpiece of knowledge for you to grow, prosper and create peace and wellbeing. During my compilation of this amazing puzzle, the question was asked of me, "Who are you without your story?" I will share my story with you throughout the book.

I had suddenly become consciously aware of all the ill effects and impact each of my life stories had on my wellbeing. I had carried them on my back for far too long and it was finally time to start off-loading some of these weights. The essential thing here is not to leave them behind and forget them—which would seem like an obvious choice—but to instead invest in them by living and learning from each and every one of them. To forget them, in my opinion, would be almost criminal—all that suffering, and

"Who are you without your story?"

for what? Better not to waste the experience, as there would be no benefit from that. Instead, I made the choice to embrace and use each one of them for future reference.

For most of you, these very events or stories, as I will refer to them, still remain unexplored burdens, or unchallenged demons. Their effects continue to cause damage to you, not just mentally but physically. The daily impact can be huge, especially when neglected and allowed to continue to fester and grow within you. Please don't underestimate the consequences of this, as they can lead to both physical and mental health issues which can ultimately destroy your relationships, not just with your loved ones, but often we forget and take them to work every day too. It's often hard to separate from them.

Basically, what I am saying is that the effects can be endless. The list of symptoms can also be infinite and often exhausting. This vital yet compelling knowledge combined with basic financial literacy skills can forever change and improve not only your wellbeing, which is paramount, but your money position. All of this is covered thoroughly in the enhanced components of my Find Your Zero™ programs, which I now deliver both online and through one-on-one coaching.

To reiterate I would ask you, "Are you are completely happy with every aspect of your life as it is right now?" If you can confidently answer yes, then I am guessing you have achieved everything you ever set out to do, wouldn't change a thing and, technically speaking, you should be really happy with your life as it is right now, right?

But are you? It appears that in our quest to keep up with our peers—or worse still, strangers—we are no longer happy with the simple things in life. Instead, we prefer to over-stretch ourselves, often resulting in juggling unwanted anxiety, stress or depression as well as relationships, children and work in the pursuit to achieve what we perceive to be financial happiness, growth or security, whatever that is for you.

By doing so, have you somehow forgotten or neglected the most vital part of the equation? *You.* Life is demanding, but is this really the path you have chosen to tread or did you just get a little lost along the way and take a wrong turn?

I have created this quote which I believe sums it all up nicely:

> *"Life is like a kaleidoscope, with every move and turn the outcome changes."*
>
> — BELINDA MANGANI

Of course, I am not suggesting that your life is bad. In fact, it's probably pretty darn good. You see, most customers I see actually believe they are doing really well and some even deny that they are in any need of assistance. That is, of course, until I dig a little deeper. Although claiming to live the high life, most eventually admit that they aren't actually living the life they envisaged for themselves many years earlier, let alone yesterday or even today.

How do you feel about the word budget and do you believe you can improve your wellbeing as a result of simply applying good money management skills?

Please be assured you are certainly not alone. In fact, the majority are right beside you in your journey and feeling exactly the same as you. Some may even say they are frustrated, tired or even exhausted at times. Is this due to your efforts in maintaining

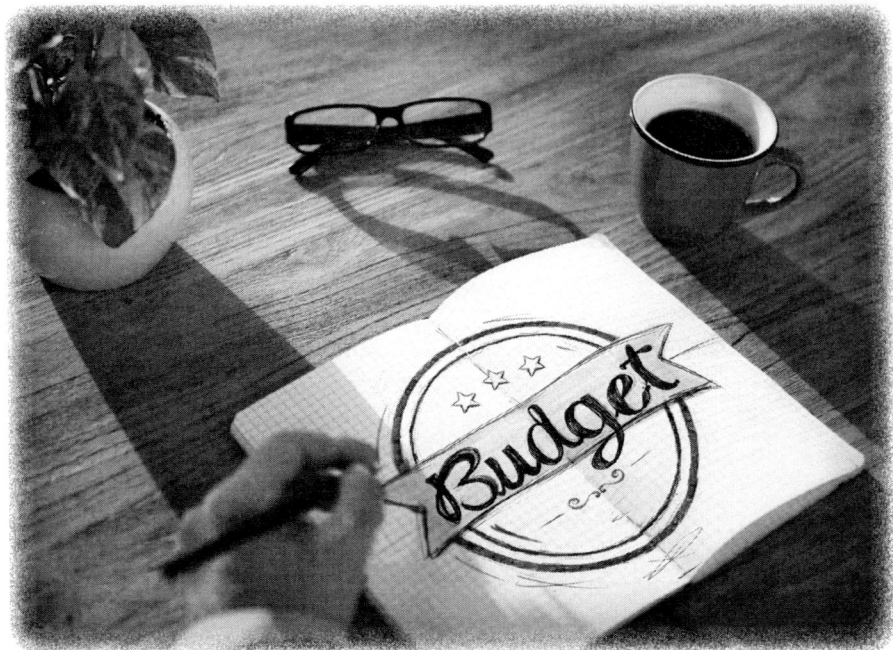

a façade for the world to see? Well, you'll be pleased to hear that there is good news. You are in the right place at the right time. If you take the chance and make a change, things won't be this way forever and better still, it's really not hard at all to improve every aspect of your life. You just need the skills and knowledge to help you get there—and that's where I fit in.

I think a good place to start is to define and understand the true meaning of these two important words that I will be use throughout my books. How do you feel about the word *budget* and do you believe you can improve your *wellbeing* as a result of simply applying good money management skills? I believe this all revolves around your perceptions of *yourself* and *your money*. You see, I realised that in creating a program that will assist you to succeed financially, first and foremost I actually needed to unfold and reveal the many components that make up the reasons why most of you don't already have a plan in place.

"Health is the greatest gift, contentment the greatest wealth, faithfulness the best relationship."

— SRI BUDDHA

In order to make this learning curve a vital part of your success, I have spent a lot of time finding easy-to-follow methods and ways to teach you, that combine both relevance and importance in order to be able to deliver this in such a way that it has a profound effect on the way that you interpret the information provided. It is my philosophy that how you interpret things ultimately impacts the end result you will achieve. Your mindset and how you nurture and grow it can significantly change and improve your life in more ways than one.

"We are what we think. All that we are arises with our thoughts. With our thoughts, we make the world."

— SRI BUDDHA

I hope that in reading this, you will understand that life is a journey and whatever you do, wherever you go, it should always be *you* that determines *your* outcome.

2

Where Does It All Start?

"Anyone who has ever asked for directions knows you need two crucial pieces of information to get good results: a starting point and a destination."

— MIKE QUIGLEY

In choosing a point to start my story, I suppose it would be remiss of me to not take you back to where my journey truly began. For me, it all started with one of the most significant events in my life, an event that has caused me a considerable amount of trauma and pain and probably one that has taken, or will take, forever to completely understand.

This leads me back to around 1973 when I was just six years of age. To be completely honest, I am not sure if I can even remember much of my younger years—maybe I blocked them out simply to survive. Of course, as you will learn in my Find Your Zero™ programs, the reason why I believe it is so vitally important to share my story with you today, is because it is what has led me to not only be the person I am today but it also provides the source and reference points for all my teachings. I really want to emphasise this because it is vital for you to understand the significance your stories are continuing to have on your personal wellbeing on a daily basis.

The truth as I see it, is that your stories not only contribute to the person you have become, but sometimes they tend to dominate and prevent you from becoming truly amazing. I realise that, although I have personally fought hard to rid myself of my stories, it is increasingly obvious to me that, as I stumble through life's challenges I constantly still come across signs that I now begin to recognise, and see their impact by the behaviours I have created along the way.

Your stories not only contribute to the person you have become, but sometimes they tend to dominate and prevent you from becoming truly amazing.

Let's wind the clock back to my six-year-old self and explore the events that took place that laid the foundations of my personal journey. My life was instantly turned upside down when I discovered that my father had left us. I was devastated, heartbroken and totally confused by my father leaving me. I could not understand what was happening and started looking to find the reasons why. Over the years I would hear people say that I was lucky that I was so young when it happened, but really, divorce has no age boundaries. Even as young as six, I struggled to understand why he had left me behind.

As harsh as it may seem, I thought it was fair enough that he had decided he no longer wanted to be married to my mother, but why did he leave *me* behind? Sure, my mother was hurting deeply too and I felt her pain as well. Maybe this somehow doubled my pain. I had so many questions as I struggled to emotionally come to terms with what was taking place. We spent what felt like forever crying, all the while trying to make sense of it all. She tried desperately hard to help me, but no matter what she said or did I still couldn't comprehend why he was able to walk away from me.

Going to school seemed like a form of punishment. We had just moved to a new house and my mother had enrolled my brother and I at the local Catholic primary school. I can still remember crying almost every day for the entire time I was at that school—I often begged her not to make me go.

There were a variety of reasons why I didn't like going to school, one of which was that I somehow felt like my teachers were singling me out because my parents were divorced or because I came from a single-parent family. Of course, back then this wasn't seen as very acceptable, especially at a Catholic school, where divorce was somewhat frowned upon, but truth be known I had so much more going on.

On top of the emotional issues I also had severe abdominal pain and constantly experienced feelings of nausea and dizziness. My mother did her very best and I know she truly wanted to believe that I was really unwell, but doctors and teachers ganged up on us, insisting that I was acting out. Occasionally, I experienced so much agonising stomach pain that she would take me to the hospital and rather than trying to diagnose me, find the cause and help me, they simply put two and two together and came up with five. They told my mother I was simply seeking her attention. I can even remember on one occasion at the hospital when that they sat me down—I think I was about eight or nine years old—and they went to great lengths to explain to me that "I had a big sausage in my stomach going round and round".

That's right—they put it all down to anxiety and stress. The pains were actually a huge *source* of my stress because I was genuinely in a huge amount of discomfort. They weren't just ignoring it, but trying their hardest to convince my mother and I that it was "all in my mind". Even though I knew it was real and not made up, somehow they had still managed to create an element of doubt in my mind and confuse me so much so that I even started to question my own sanity. I wondered whether it was possible that I actually had the power to bring on these symptoms. I constantly found myself beginning to question whether the pain was real or if in fact it was as a result of my emotional state. I knew I was traumatised by losing my father, there was no doubting that—but the pain?

I can still clearly remember having a tug-of-war outside my front door, when my lovely Catholic school teachers turned up at my home before school one day, insisting I attend and that if my mother didn't bring me, they would. They grabbed me by the arm. I looked back at my mother for support, tears streaming down my face. They yelled at her, saying that if she didn't bring me to school they would call the truancy officer. She promptly and confidently shouted back, "Okay, do that!" and took me back inside. Looking back now, my mother is only 20 years older than me so at 28 she was still almost a child herself, dealing with her own trauma of losing her husband and now being forced to having to deal with these awful teachers, all the while probably wondering whether I was telling her the truth. Years later she told me that she always wanted to believe me, and did, but the doctors did present a compelling theory filled with what seemed like real facts—that all seemed to stack up against me.

Every day presented a real and ongoing challenge as I tried desperately to manage my pain without understanding what was causing it. I totally admit that, on top of my stomach pains and other symptoms, there was no doubting that I was also suffering from the anguish of living without my father. I found myself doing strange things like hiding for what seemed like forever under my bed in the hope that someone would notice I was missing and come

As I grew up I wanted so desperately to fill the gap in my life with love.

looking for me, but I always seemed to give up waiting well before it ever became noticeable. I used to contemplate running away, but never did, because I always saw the consequences first. All these things ran around in my head but never eventuated.

I also constantly found myself plagued with suicidal thoughts but again thought through the possibilities of what could go wrong, which ultimately prevented any attempts—I always imagined the what-ifs first. What if I ended up worse off than I am now? Thankfully, logic always won the game. As I grew up I wanted so desperately to fill the gap in my life with love. Even though I had a fabulous family life, surrounded by loving relatives, something always seemed to be missing. As I moved into my teen years, depression became a big part of who I was but would float in and out, leading me to question whether it was a chemical imbalance rather than anything else.

When my father left us, he let us stay in the house. I guess he thought this was an amazing gesture of kindness on his behalf, but in fact it was a huge mortgage that my mother was determined to conquer. She sought work wherever she could, but financially it was challenging. I remember having to get both myself and my brother ready in the mornings and walking us both to school, stopping on the way to do up his shoe laces up and mothering him, as you do when you're the elder sibling. I have such fond memories of us together and we were best friends. I hated what had happened to me, to us, and constantly challenged and sought answers, trying forever to find the *why*. I am sure this made my life all that more difficult, but it's me and this is who I am. Being the responsible child that I was, I took on the role of helper. I know that my mother was always so respectful of me and knew of my constant struggles to cope, but sometimes she needed to allocate some tasks to me just to survive. I found myself stressing all day about these jobs, such as taking the mortgage money to school, worrying about getting to the bank on time, losing the money—you name it, I did it.

This also prevented me from concentrating completely and doing well at school. It stopped me just being a kid. Instead it manifested itself within me, causing me pain and anxiety. I was constantly sick, suffering from stomach pains, vertigo and headaches. I often wondered myself if the doctors were right in saying that my symptoms were self-inflicted, as a result of the constant pressures and responsibility that I was simply too young to handle. My mother says now that she had little choice but to delegate to me; that she felt I was the kind of child that was mature and able to handle it— but what if I wasn't? What if I was carefree, easy going, incapable of responsibility? What if I'd lost the mortgage money on the way to school or just forgotten to pay it? What then?

I barely slept at night all those years. I hated the darkness that night-time brought with it. I had to check all the cupboard doors were closed, to look under my bed, constantly feeling a presence around me in that house. Honestly, I hated that house; to me it felt haunted and I guess this added to my already crazy, out-of-control life. Mind you, decades later my mother would confess to me that she had actually been shook whilst lying asleep in her own room. Some of you may be thinking it all seems unbelievable. I kid you not when I say I have been exposed to a huge array of events and occurrences, providing me with not just an insight into feelings but a full comprehension of the kinds of traumas that may have led you to your life events and stories.

High school brought with it an opportunity for a new start around new kids, as most were going onto the Catholic secondary school, whilst I was off to the local high school. I made myself a promise— no more crying—and kept to it pretty well. I did, however, continue to miss quite a bit of school over the years due to illness, so keeping friends also seemed like a task in itself. It seemed like nobody wanted to have a friend that was there one day and gone the next. My mother was young, so we enjoyed each other's company. To some degree she became a part of my friendship group—not intentionally on her behalf. We just seemed to get along well.

I managed to make friends with two girls and the three of us formed a great bond. One didn't have many other friends—she was a size 24 at the age of 13—and the other was very shy. Together we made an awesome team. I guess I had finally found my place and they accepted me for who I was. On reflection, I now see that we each played a significant role in each other's lives. I was their protector, warning off all the attackers that constantly seemed to want to put them down. In return, they loved me unconditionally, devotedly sitting on the bench seat awaiting my arrival each day. I felt comfortable in their presence and could shine, and likewise, I hope that they would be able to look back now and see the role that I played.

So, by now I was 14 and my mother wanted to go back to school and finish her education. Once again, being the child that I was, I took on the role of encouraging and supporting her and felt pleased to do so. Over the years I'd been nurtured and trained in this role and by now I was quite good at it.

By the age of 16 I had successfully completed a secretarial course as part of my Year 11 certificate and I was ready to face the big world—I was excited. Luckily enough, with some interview skills practiced at home, I managed to convince a big law firm to take me on and so began my working career as a private secretary in the city. I was now making my own money and with it came a real sense of not just financial freedom, but the feeling that I could be and do anything. Having grown up in a single-parent family with little or no money, this now brought about a whole new aspect of life. I could finally afford to start buying myself the little things that I had felt I missed out on watching others around me wearing brand-name clothes. My mother had made most, if not all of my clothes. I even said to her once, "Thank God you can't make shoes." I could now buy myself chips and lollies anytime I wanted. Money opened up a whole new world of lovely things.

> *My dream had become a goal. I hadn't given up on the dream, but rather created a bigger financial objective.*

I decided I wanted to buy my own stereo system, a three-in-one. How funny does that sound now? It had a radio, cassette player and small speakers. I remember going with my mother to a big electronics store and making a bee-line straight for the $400 system that I had saved for. I turned it on with sheer excitement. I just felt great to have saved enough money to buy it. But the salesman who said, "Well, if you think that sounds good, come over here and listen to this one," ended up feeling even better.

$1,600 later, at four times the original price, I was sold. I had walked into the store to buy and he had up-sold me instantly. There was no way I could listen to the horrible hollow sound that crappy $400 three-in-one was pumping out after I had heard that refined and magnificent Yamaha system. I turned and looked at my mother and she said those magical words every kid loves to hear, especially at 16. "Well thank you, but she only has $400 saved up so she will need to go home and save some more, then we'll be back". I couldn't believe my ears; my mother had just completely crushed my dreams of ever owning a great sound system. I left the store with tears in my eyes that day.

For some, this would have presented an opportunity to take out the finance to buy it on the spot, which goes completely against my grain. Another alternative was to simply to give up on the dream. Instead, I chose to make a plan to achieve it and calculated exactly how much I would need to save each week to get back there as quickly as possible and get *my* stereo. My dream had become a goal. I hadn't given up on the dream, but rather created a bigger financial objective. Immediately I went home and every week I got my pay I put aside the amount I needed. Three months later, I returned to that same electronics store and purchased that wonderful Yamaha system—with cold, hard cash.

It was a big, multi-level sound system contained in a black cabinet with two-smoked glass doors and waist-high speakers, one at either side. The first layer was the turntable with a nice shiny plastic lid that lifted up so you could play vinyl records. The second layer had an AM/FM radio, the third a double cassette deck and the fourth an equaliser. Finally, at the bottom was a rack for placing your records. You can only imagine how proud I felt leaving the store that day with all those huge boxes, ready to assemble the first of many dreams and goals that I would have throughout my life.

And it didn't stop there. In fact, this set a precedent for what I could achieve moving forward. I continued to set aside money as I went about creating my next major financial goal. I guess it was a normal progression. Most kids talk about getting a car, although these days it is sad to see parents taking out personal loans and giving their kids cars. It would have been nice to drive and own a car but I simply hadn't saved enough. The hardest part was watching my friends get their own cars, but they were different to me. There were borrowing the money, taking out personal loans and paying them off monthly, whereas for me, I had been taught that if you can't afford to pay cash then you really can't have it, simple as that. I heard all the stories from my mother; if you borrow the money, you will need to pay extra interest yet the car would only go down in value.

It made perfect sense. It was better to save the interest and use all that extra money towards buying a better car. By 19, I'd got my license and saved $7,000 to buy my first car, It was a six-year-old Ford Cortina 1979 model with only 40,000 kilometres on the clock. My friends had borrowed $3,000 and after three years their cars were only worth around $1,500. And now they owed more than the car was actually worth. Life was cruising along nicely, I had the freedom to go where I wanted in my own car and generally speaking, I was happy. But was I?

I was still feeling a little lost. I had a job but I hated it; the boss was an absolutely disgusting person, abusing me constantly, but again, I listened to my mother who told me, "Belinda you need to build a good working history—you can't just change jobs." So, I stayed and continued to tolerate the abuse day after day. The boss was a barely five-foot-tall, thirty-something lawyer with a shoulder-length mullet and he thought he was tough stuff, only at the expense of others. He continued to demean and destroy the confidence of all the younger staff members. I guess in hindsight it gave him power and made him feel important—he seriously needs to get on top of his story, don't you think?

At 19, my next major hurdle occurred with the passing of my beloved Opa (my mother is Dutch) and with that went a huge part of me. He had represented the father figure in my life that I never had and now that was gone too. I had hit rock bottom, thinking, "Why is it that every man I love is taken away from me?" And with it came that stupid "Why me?" question yet again. Now, I realise for some of you this all might sound insignificant and I truly appreciate that my struggles may not seem that bad, considering there is so much real tragedy in the world, but please understand that for me

One day, out of the blue, I bought myself a round-the-world ticket and off I went.

this was devastating. Once again I found myself struggling to make sense of my life. I fell into a state of depression after his death and again wondered whether life in fact had anything special in store for me. Frankly, at that point I didn't feel life was worth continuing.

Of course, there were other little things going on, too many to mention, but all of this culminated in negative ways of thinking.

I struggled daily to deal with the constant questions running around in my head. "Why does all this bad shit keep happening to me?" I realise that these moments happen to each and every one of us, but at that moment I felt like it was singling me out. I seemed to be surrounded by generally happy people moving through life but there I was going nowhere. My mother gathered a few people around from her prayer group and, reluctantly, I let them pray over me. The words that came were, "Something good is just around the corner." I sat there patiently, eyes closed, thinking *if it makes them feel better I will just go along with it.*

The next day I got up for work and as I walked to the station at 7am the roads were quiet—there wasn't a soul in sight. That particular day I struggled more than usual fighting to hold back the tears. Suddenly, from nowhere, appeared an old man on a bicycle. "Good morning, beautiful!" he said, with a cheer in his voice as he rode past me. I immediately turned around but to my surprise there was no one in sight. Not a soul. "Could this be a sign?" I asked as I gathered myself together. Was it possible that I imagined him? It doesn't really matter—it had worked and I had the strength once again to soldier on.

Years later, aged 25, having finally changed jobs (a few times) moving closer and closer to home, I finally decided it was time. Time to travel the world. One day, out of the blue, I bought myself a round-the-world ticket and off I went. It was to be a journey of self-discovery, learning to find myself and finally work out what I wanted to do. Keep in mind I had only ever really only been to the shops and work by myself, so this was a huge leap of faith. Unfortunately, I was the only one who had saved enough money and so with $25,000 I embarked on the journey alone. It was enough for a house deposit and being the responsible person I was the thought had definitely crossed my mind, but I was at a point in my life where I desperately needed to find myself. I had so many dreams and aspirations but felt as though I was getting nowhere in life.

I remember getting to my first stop, Hong Kong, and thinking *oh my God, I can't do this.* There I was, in a foreign country surrounded by what seemed to be an overwhelming lack of English—I was scared. I called home. Thankfully, my mother and brother both said, "Keep going, you can do it." And so I pushed myself. Nine months later and twenty-something kilos heavier, I returned home. Honestly, the moment I landed I just wanted to say "Hi" and turn around and get back on the plane, but I didn't. My mother hugged me, trying desperately not to cry as she looked at my now very overweight body. "Don't worry," she proclaimed. "I will take you home and get that weight off you."

Prior to gaining all the extra weight, even at 5'10" and 67 kilos, I had always been told, "If you lost a few kilos you would look great." Here I was now at 90kg and for the first time I was really me. On my quest to find myself I had discovered a new strength. This didn't alter the fact that I hated the way I looked, and constantly felt the need to remind not just myself, but everyone I met of how I was usually much skinner. What I discovered was more interesting. I personally felt I had become a better person inside, yet when I ran into people I knew before I put on the weight, they turned the other way, pretending not to know this fat person before them. My family still loved me unconditionally. I couldn't help but think, "What the heck?" I thought, "What? I'm not good enough to speak to now because I'm fat?" By eating sensibly again, the weight quickly started dropping off and I returned to 75kg, where I started to feel normal again.

Through this, I learnt so much about myself as a person, but also other people and their perceptions of me. During that time I realised how most of us tend to judge people based on their appearance alone. Funny enough, as I lost the weight those very same people now suddenly wanted to renew our friendship—it was too late. I had seen them for what they really were; I was moving forward as a person and wanted nothing more to do with them. I had also learnt how to love myself and being alone was no longer a concern of mine.

I was 26 and ready to settle down and have a family of my own. I didn't want to waste any time finding the right person. I needed to reflect on everything I had now learnt in life. To find a life partner I needed to not only be strict but precise about what I truly needed in a partner, so I began to make a list of the core values and qualities my perfect husband would need to have. My list went a little like this: non-smoker, no children or previous marriages (divorce was rather a taboo subject for me) must want children, must be a Christian, must believe marriage is forever, must have a secure job, have a good sense of humour and—I guess most importantly—must love me for who I am.

I realised how most of us tend to judge people based on their appearance alone.

The easy part done, I was off to find Mr. Right. Unbelievably, I could never have imagined that in such a short time, I would find him. After only a few months of being home, I met Frank, my husband of 25 years. Six weeks after our first date, he proposed. We had a small family gathering to celebrate our engagement and ten weeks later we got married. I think my list had served me well. Except one thing I should have put on the list: "Must be a good talker." I forgot that one, and although he is perfect in every other way it would be great if he would talk just a little more. I guess that's not bad going— and I am far from perfect myself.

CHAPTER

3

How My Passion Turned To Money Management

"Ours is a divine journey; therefore, this journey has neither a beginning nor an end... This journey has a goal, but it does not stop at any goal, for it has come to realise that today's goal is only the starting point of tomorrow's journey."

— SRI CHINMOY

In 1992 at age 26, I met and married my husband. It was a whirlwind romance as you just heard in the previous chapter. We met in June, got engaged in July and married on 8 November 1992. I must tell you my husband Frank is the polar opposite of me, or as one person accurately pointed out we are ying and yang, perfectly balanced. I quite like that analogy.

When we got married my new husband said to me, "Belinda you have two choices, you can either work for the rest of your life and have whatever you want, or if you want to be a stay at home mum with kids you need to first help pay off the house, because on one wage it would be impossible".

For me the answer was instantly clear. We would need to pay off the house as quickly as possible and then I could comfortably be a stay at home Mum. Given my new goal it didn't take long for me to create our new **Money Plan**, quickly mapping out timeframes and creating a new Money Plan that would enable us to pay off the mortgage as soon as possible. Actually thinking back, we didn't for one moment think we were in the mortgage for a 30 year payback plan, no way not even 10 years. I quickly came back with our four (4) year plan. That's correct only four years and the house would be paid off enabling me to quit my job, stay at home, be a Mum and have fun raising our children, the rest just seemed like history.

Life was as perfect as we could ever have imagined it could be. Not only did we own our own home, we now also had our dream three beautiful, healthy children and a second property.

Fast-forward only four years later, and yes the mortgage was done and dusted.

In 1998, our first child, a son, was born and then in 2001, our twin daughters were born. Life was as perfect as we could ever have imagined it could be. Not only did we own our own home, we now also had our dream three beautiful, healthy children and a second property, also in Williamstown, the mortgage of which was now down to about half, around $65,000.

Despite all of this, I was at home raising children and although we were asset-rich, we were cash-poor. I loved being a mum but realised I wasn't as good at cooking and cleaning as I had hoped I would be and wanted to do something more mind-stimulating, still staying at home during the day. I knew that if we had just a little bit of extra income things would be easier, so I took jobs at night while the kids were in bed, but they were boring jobs. I have never been good at repetitive work and found it challenging to keep going to these jobs.

In 2004, with three children under the age of six, my mother called me. She had seen an advertisement from Aussie Home Loans. They were a large company seeking mortgage brokers. She suggested that with my knowledge of loans and money that I should consider applying. She believed I would make a really good mortgage broker. I had no previous work experience in the banking field, but what I did possess was a strong desire and passion to make a difference in the lives of others who were struggling to make sense of banking and lending criteria. We owned everything we had, we didn't have any debts, yet were unable to borrow money ourselves as the bank said we didn't earn enough. I wondered how it could be that we were able to save, go on great holidays and have enough money, with a pool of assets, yet we didn't qualify to borrow money. I applied and I got the job. As part of the setup process, I had to come up with a name for my new company, as I would be sole director and self-employed for the first time ever. It was an exciting time.

After a great deal of deliberation, I finally decided on a name for my new company, one that I believed would truly reflect my passion: "Building Blocks for the Future." For me, the name represented everything that I wanted to achieve. I saw it as a unique opportunity, one that I believed would allow me to become responsible for helping the community to build a better financial future and, at the same time, giving me the opportunity to educate and empower people with skills and knowledge that would enable them to help put themselves in a better financial position and ultimately qualify for loans.

> *I had no previous work experience in the banking field, but what I did possess was a strong desire and passion to make a difference in the lives of others who were struggling to make sense of banking and lending criteria.*

I read this quote and I love it; Bob Hope said, "A bank is an institution that will lend you money when you can prove that you don't need it." What does that mean? When you have a job, and everything is going well for you, typically you don't need to borrow more money, unless you are adding to your asset pool. On the flip side when things go wrong, they usually go terribly wrong and that's when you need more money, to keep you afloat to see you through the tough times and keep you from losing everything. However, this is usually at a time when you have either lost your job, suffered an illness, are looking after a family member who desperately needs your help or something you have invested in has failed. Most, if not all, are contributing factors that are usually not by choice and you have little or no control over them. Retrospectively, had you known any of these situations would occur, you would have surely borrowed or saved a little harder to provide yourself with a buffer.

Years later, now equipped with a Certificate IV and Diploma in Finance and Mortgage Broking Management, specialising in home lending for first home buyers and investors alike, I noticed that most of my customers all seemed to have common financial positions, regardless of value or level of income. Of course, there were the exceptions, but customers contacting a mortgage broker were typically those that the banks had rejected, or couldn't borrow as much as they would have liked. Most, if not all, were given little or no reason as to why they were declined. Frustrated and annoyed, they were seeking answers. An important, yet generally overlooked factor, was that none of my customers had ever missed a payment and none were in arrears. Most were earning enough money, yet going backwards financially. Their lack of understanding as to why they had been declined arose from the fact that they were all able to afford to pay larger repayments on higher-end debts such as credit cards and personal loans.

Often, people were calling simply because they did not "fit the box". By this I mean they did not meet the bank's lending criteria and they didn't understand why. I also noticed that there wasn't anybody in the community teaching or showing people how to get out of debt and none of the banks or lenders were explaining to customers why they didn't qualify.

Why was it that they could afford all their existing debts and yet they could not consolidate or refinance their credit cards, car loans and/or personal loans into their lowest-interest product— their home loan? A common question seemed to always be, "Why did we get knocked back when we tried to consolidate?" The big hype amongst their friendship groups was to consolidate all your debts into one. That way you are only paying home loan rates on your expensive credit card debts. It certainly made sense to them, and they couldn't understand why they were being declined. What they failed to see was that most of them owed more than they were worth. In most cases, their debts exceeded their total net worth. So while affordability in terms of their debts was there, the security that they were offering to the bank was not.

A common question seemed to always be, "Why did we get knocked back when we tried to consolidate?"

This led me to think again about what I was teaching people, reflecting on what we had done ourselves that was so different. Most of my new clients were earning far more than us and yet achieving only half as much. I began documenting my processes and turning these into workshops that have made a significant difference to the lives of so many already. The solution wasn't simply borrowing more, but rather managing what they had better. I found myself searching for a name that I felt best described what I could do for others. This name would represent what my customers needed to do to make changes. **"Find Your Zero"** was born and while it made no sense to some of my closest friends, customers started calling and saying, "I'm excited to find my zero," and thanking me for helping them. Finally, I'd found a name that I believe represented the correlation between an individual and their money. I heard one person say, "Who wants to find *zero*? That can't be a good thing?" You need to trust me when I say you need to find where your zero is to become totally debt free.

You are seeking not just your financial zero but your personal zero as well. As more and more people called to book a one-day workshop with me, I quickly realised that I would not be able to fit so many into my calendar and decided to have a website built that could deliver an online version of the course. This would not only keep the costs for participants down and achieve a process of delivery that could reach anyone anywhere in the world, but it could also provide a way of sharing a message of financial hope and personal growth with not just people in close proximity but to the greater community—maybe even the world. Finally, this would enable me to deliver a fun, interactive, customer-

> *The solution wasn't simply borrowing more, but rather managing what they had better.*

friendly support system that could benefit many, especially those needing immediate assistance.

The greatest problem I then faced was coming to terms with charging a fee to help people when they were already struggling financially to pay all their bills. The answer to that came from my customer Marissa, who said to me:

"Belinda, your course has paid for itself already. In only a few short weeks we have learned to save, and those savings have put us in front of where we started three weeks ago. We are now moving forward quickly. Thank you—we could not have done it on our own. You have saved our finances, our relationship and helped us as a family to become closer. We are so glad we made that call to you."

I couldn't find a bigger compliment than this. My work was already making a significant difference—and so this book was born.

4

Fix Your Life, Not Just Your Money

"You are your greatest asset. Put your time, effort and money into training, grooming, and encouraging your greatest asset."

— TOM HOPKINS

After working with families and individuals over a 20-year period, and particularly in the past 14 years since I became an accredited mortgage broker, I started to see patterns emerging that would constantly lead me to ask myself, "Are all my customers alike?" And if they are, what is it that they all have in common? What is that all-important commonality that prevents or hinders many of my customers from achieving financial success?

In order to find the answers to those burning questions, I quickly started going over them case-by-case in my mind, to piece together the similarities that they all had, so I could share these compelling and very powerful revelations with you in my books in the hope that they will help you unlock the answers you seek. However, in doing this exercise, I needed to ask myself the very same, all-important yet dreaded question: "Am I exactly the same as all my customers?" This would ultimately hold the answer to that burning dilemma facing all of my customers: "Why can't we ever seem to get out of debt?"

> *I think most of us would like to believe that the answer is simple—that it's completely in the numbers.*

So, I hope at this point you are saying, "Please tell me what you discovered, and help me solve my financial problems." As I hinted earlier, if I had told you that this book would include digging deep into yourself and examining your soul to help you make personal revelations about yourself or your life, would you be here today or would you simply have shrugged off the idea that there could be a link between your story and your financial well-being?

I think most of us would like to believe that the answer is simple— that it's completely in the numbers. I hate to be the bearer of bad news, but it's not. Whilst the ability to play the numbers game is a skill that you may want, or have now chosen to learn, it alone will not ease the task of paying your bills. This tends to be a big challenge for a lot of my customers, even those earning mega-bucks. Often, the consensus is that if you could just outsource the task of managing your money and/or debt to a so-called professional, this would somehow miraculously stretch your dollar further.

Now, I'm not suggesting that this doesn't work for some. Listening to the constant radio and TV commercials offering such a service, it must surely work for some, but for the majority I think it's fair to say that the belief behind this strategy is that it will somehow eliminate the need for you to change; that you can continue living your life without the need for modification. Somehow everything is going to improve for you simply by giving away control over your money. Well, sign me up—sounds like a great plan!

But is it truly possible for a stranger to come along and pay all your bills with the same amount of money when you couldn't? This is a fee-for-service option and with it comes attached a regular fee that you will almost certainly need to pay indefinitely if you aren't going to modify your spending or change the way you think. I don't believe it's possible to make sufficient changes without gaining the personal skills or knowledge of money management, and by choosing this option you must accept the fact that you will become reliant upon others forever. I know you wouldn't be sacrificing your valuable time reading this if you thought that was a viable option. Giving up responsibility or control of your life and/or money does not change the facts. My aim for you is to empower yourself so that you never have to be completely reliant upon others, especially when it comes to your hard-earned money.

Initially, most of my customers are a little hesitant, and rightly so. They believe that I will suggest that they give up all or most of the things they enjoy. Alternatively, they think that I will just suggest that they spend less or, on the flip-side, I will simply tell them to get another job—work more to earn more. While all of this seems like an obvious answer, and to some extent it is, it's simply not as easy to put these practices into place. They don't provide a realistic solution or even change the bigger picture. For the majority, unless you have a job that allows you to work more shifts permanently, how does one simply start earning more overnight? I don't see simply earning more as a realistic option for most, short or long-term. What about someone who is self-employed? It's the desire to improve or reach a goal that often determines whether extra work is attainable, even though it may prove to be worthwhile financially.

If what I've discovered is even minutely relevant, and if your story has a bearing on your success or failure, be it financial or not, then simply handing over your money to an expert will not provide you with a solution, let alone a long-term plan. What I typically see is that you will simply revert back to what you know. Put into simple terms, if you can't pay all your bills with the money you are currently bringing home, regardless of the source of that income, then nobody else will be able to pay them for you either, regardless of their skills or expertise. Trust me when I say that if you don't have enough money, outsourcing the problem will not change it for the better; quite the contrary, as you will now have extra to pay—their fees.

On the other hand, I have met many customers who have told me that, despite being able to successfully pay all their bills, they have been drawn into believing ideas that seemed to provide viable solutions, only to find that they have involved extending their current loan term in order to reduce their repayments, or in extreme situations, bankruptcy has been suggested as a recommended and viable alternative. This option has much longer and often devastating effects, not just on finances but also on relationships. While I am not claiming that these options are always unavoidable, in a lot of cases, it has not been the best option offered, but rather a means of generating income for companies specialising in debt consolidation or reduction. In saying this, I know the same rule cannot be applied across the board, as I have heard the minority saying that it has been good for them.

In times of extreme stress and desperation we are all vulnerable and often misguided, without even being aware of alternatives, and left feeling our choices are limited. I once received a call from a telemarketer trying to sell me advertising space and, after a long conversation, she poured her heart out to me, saying that she wished she had heard of my service earlier. She explained to me that she and her husband had a loan that they could manage and afford. However, they sought assistance as they wished they had more funds available each month so that they didn't need to struggle living week-to-week, worrying and arguing about bills all the time. She informed me that they had utilised the services of a debt consolidator (they didn't have a house to use as collateral) who initially seemed to achieve their objectives by successfully renegotiating all of their loans into one. She explained that their repayments each month had decreased but when I asked her, "Did your loan go from three years to seven years?" she replied, "How did you know?" I said it's common practice—that's how they can reduce your repayments.

I asked her whether she was able to pay extra to reduce the loan to which she said yes. What confused her most was that they now owed far more. How could this be? I explained to her that the process of renegotiating the term of their loan involves a fee. In other words, the company offering the service has added their fee into the new loan amount by renegotiating and extending the loan period. She was shocked, as she wasn't aware there was such a big fee involved. Unfortunately, in times of desperation the fine print doesn't always appear clear and your vision is often clouded by the opportunity to provide a quick, band-aid solution to your problem, often realising the extent of the damage when it's too late. Given that most customers would not be in a position to proceed with the suggested plan if they first had to pay the set fee, this is a way of the company guaranteeing their fee for service, while also providing the customer with a means to an end as well. But what if there was a better way to achieve a reduction in your debts without paying such a huge amount of money?

Sadly, she went on to explain that they could afford to pay the original amount and sometimes even more, but it felt uncomfortable and they just wanted some breathing space. Now their debt was drawn out for an even longer period and that she deeply regretted taking that option. The biggest problem with most customers, as mentioned above, is the fact that they don't have money. They are already struggling with debt so how can they pay to fix their problem? For most, like I just explained, the fee is added to their existing loan, the term is extended, and this is seen to be a solution, but is it a good solution? In some instances—I hate to say it—but yes, it can provide a solution. However, this raises the more important questions like, "Can you renegotiate on your own?" Absolutely. So why don't most people do that? Firstly, they don't know that it's an option; secondly, they are so mentally and physically drained by the stress and pressure that they don't know where to begin. So, where am I going with all this?

If you don't identify and correct what the underlying problem is that is causing you to constantly fall behind, then no matter how good the expert is that's looking after your money, you won't always get ahead. It's that good old band-aid effect that I mentioned before—and we all know how that turns out. I often say, "What happens to a band-aid if you jump in a pool?" Typically, it comes off, right? Someone once said to me, "Belinda, you aren't just a numbers person, anyone can put numbers on a page. You are a mindset person and not everybody has that skill—this is what makes you different to most financial experts." Finally, it all seemed to start making sense. I could start to connect what I had worked on for so long, developing a positive mindset to change the outcome of not-so-positive experiences into valuable learning experiences—and connect that to money.

> *"Can you renegotiate on your own?" Absolutely. So why don't most people do that?*

So, what exactly is mindset? Our mindset is created and made up of a series of thoughts, beliefs and values, some of which are true but, more importantly, some we simply believe to be true, but aren't necessarily correct. These essentially affect everything we do and impact our lives on a daily basis. Their contribution can be interpreted either positively or negatively. However, it is our responsibility to understand the impact and the damage it may be causing to our success in life. Let's clarify firstly what I mean by using a word such as success, and what it refers to in this context.

Success should mean being happy with where we are in life. Herein lays the first real problem. Most of us measure success by comparing ourselves with the person next door, rather than simply asking ourselves, "Do I like my life?" "Am I where I want to be?" and, "If I died tomorrow, would I have regrets as to how I chose to live my life?" I would love for you to be able to say yes to all those questions but unfortunately, I know you are here right now because you have unanswered questions and your life probably isn't where you would like it to be.

> *If you don't identify and correct what the underlying problem is that is causing you to constantly fall behind, then no matter how good the expert is that's looking after your money, you won't always get ahead.*

When we begin to align our mindset with the daily activities we love to do, along with being in the presence of positive, like-minded people, the outcomes automatically start to take on a whole new meaning. I only have to look at my Find Your Zero ™ coaching programs to see that I have finally aligned who I am with what I love, and the results speak for themselves. An extra bonus is seeing how it changes the lives of those that have participated. It is such a pleasure to share in their journey.

5

What Will Your Money Journey Look Like?

"A bank is a place where they lend you an umbrella in fair weather and ask for it back when it begins to rain."

— ROBERT FROST

The phone rang and a softly spoken woman at the other end said, "Hi, Belinda. You don't know me but I got your number from a happy customer of yours who said you helped them tremendously, so I was wondering if I could book a workshop date with you?" "Of course," I said, and we locked the date in for a few days later. Normally I would ask a few more questions during the initial conversation but I sensed the quiver in her voice and felt her fragility—now was not the time to ask. A few nights later, I jumped into my car not really knowing what to expect. I plugged her address into the GPS to get the exact house location right and off I went on the 30-minute drive to her home. I was a little curious, as I knew the street name well; it was one of those streets that has huge homes and large blocks not often seen in the inner suburbs of Melbourne.

I arrived at their home and drove up the long and winding gravel driveway to a grand home. I couldn't help but wonder what had happened for them to call me that day. All the neighbouring homes had large, perfectly manicured gardens but theirs was clearly incomplete. As I got out of the car, I could hear dogs barking, which put me on guard. Promptly, the garage roller door came up and a lovely, sweet couple came out to greet me. I know never to judge a book by its cover, but again I couldn't stop myself from wondering why I was there.

I was quickly welcomed into their large, immaculately presented home and almost felt a little envious of its enormity—our home was only a portion of its size. It was lovely, uncluttered and very quiet. I began by introducing myself and asked them how I could assist. I didn't expect the story that would unfold. Most of my customers were typically earning good money and overspending, so it came as somewhat of a shock to be asked to help someone who was suffering severe financial hardship due to a workplace injury, which had resulted in a long and drawn out court case.

My heart broke for Leah and Martin as they told me their heart-breaking story. Their journey began years earlier while they were building a successful carpentry business. Everything had been going well for them and money was finally starting to come in, when suddenly one day, out of the blue, Martin slipped and fell over at work. His back was injured so badly that he was deemed unable to ever be able to return to work. Leah, on the other hand, had always had the luxury of being a stay-at-home mum but she was now forced to look for work to try and support the family's increasing financial burden. Having not been in the workplace for so long meant that she suddenly found herself struggling to find work and decided to retrain.

Worse still, time was not a luxury they could afford. Leah needed money and she needed it fast. They explained to me how the bank had forced them to sell off almost all of their assets in an attempt to save the family home from being foreclosed. Liquidating the company and its assets provided temporary relief but they soon found themselves struggling to make enough to cover their own home loan repayments, largely due to having to pay legal and medical bills on top of their home loan. My heart sank for them. Having previously worked for solicitors in personal injury claims, I knew all too well that their legal battle was far from over. I'm sure my anguish was clearly visible in my eyes as tears welled up. I struggled to hold my pain for them inside as I continued to listen to their story, all the while trying to think of a solution to help them save their home.

I explained to them that my online courses and workshops are designed to assist people work out how much they are spending versus how much they're earning—a term I refer to as "find your zero". Together, we create a money plan to reduce debts quickly and start saving. I apologised and said that I could not take their money, as my program did not properly cater for their personal situation. I didn't know if there was anything I could do to assist them, despite my empathy for their predicament.

They pleaded with me, insisting, "Surely there must be something you can do to help us. We are desperate—nobody else will help us!" They explained to me that they had been to see financial counsellors and the like but were unable to obtain any real assistance. They asked me to stay and have coffee, so I did. And so, the saga began.

If I was going to do anything for them, I first needed to do an extensive search through all their paperwork. I looked through their loan statements and bills in the hope that I could find something, anything that could make their finances easier.

My primary focus was on their wellbeing. Martin, although injured, seemed to be coping okay. However, I could sense the stress mounting within Leah. During the time I spent at their home that evening, I could see she was unable to control her trembling hands. It was evident that the damage of the ongoing stress, brought on by the constant reminder that their home was at risk of foreclosure, was unstoppable. As we sat at their table that night, I watched on, feeling helpless as she tried to maintain her composure.

Often, it's these emotions that pose the biggest danger. They are also the ones that are often left behind for whatever reason it may be—shame, guilt, embarrassment, all the above. Even the cost of treatments can affect our decision whether to seek help or not.

For this very reason, I have chosen to open my heart and share my story with you. Those of you who know me personally will know that I pride myself on being open and honest. At times, probably a little too sensitive, especially when I see others in pain. My heart truly breaks. It would defy everything that I stand for if I were to pretend that my knowledge did not come from what I have personally experienced. I am human, just like you—I struggle at times. The difference lies in my ability to pick myself up, dust off, learn and grow from every experience, good or bad. I will never make any claims to be a doctor of any kind. My story should serve as a reference guide only.

You will also see that a focal point of this book will be the often-hidden consequences that money problems can mask. Money problems can also arise at any time, from an event such as a failed investment or even illness. Someone may be prevented from working or need to give up their job to look after a partner or child. This too can lead to an array of symptoms, which can include depression, stress, anxiety or eating disorders—of which there are so many like binge eating, over-eating or even a failure to eat at all.

> *You will also see that a focal point of this book will be the often-hidden consequences that money problems can mask.*

Relationships can suffer too, not just because of a lack of money, but also differing money opinions, values or spending habits. Often overlooked is the fact that an employee may be suffering from money stress at home, which may greatly affect that person's work performance or ability to function effectively in the workplace. Ultimately, any of these issues can result in even more stress as job security is vital in maintaining a source of income that pays the bills. It can be a vicious cycle—one feeding off the other.

In fact, I would say the main reason for writing this book is because I have found that a high percentage of the clients I see are generally experiencing one or more of the above symptoms, for whatever reason. On further examination, I believe the symptoms are actually the root cause of their money problem. However, they have failed to detect it, missing the initial warning signs. Then it becomes easier to simply blame the money problem as the root cause when, in fact, it was the consequence that pushed them to seek assistance, not the actual cause.

Most people are living beyond their means, masking life's every day issues with spending. Some are aware of it; others deny it until they are finally forced to admit the truth. Unfortunately, just being aware is not a cure—ultimately, change is the only answer. Often, seeking the appropriate help also serves to add to an already stressful situation, as it involves admitting out loud that there is a problem—that you've made mistakes.

Imagine this: you've just had a really stressful day at work. You arrive at home feeling totally exhausted, flop onto the couch and the last thing you feel like doing is cooking dinner. Fair enough. I think it would be unrealistic to say that most of us haven't experienced this. You reach out, pick up the phone and call for a home delivery, or you muster up the energy to spruce yourself up and go out for dinner—sounding familiar? Ok, now let's look at the flip side. You just had the most amazing day, the boss loved your work, you got a pay rise or a bonus—I think you get my drift. You arrive home, you are bursting with excitement. You say, "Let's go out and celebrate!" Come on, admit it—we're all guilty of this too. My point is, regardless of the position we find ourselves in, win or lose, the outcome is generally the same. These days we have all become accustomed to rewarding ourselves for everything, regardless of whether it's disappointment or a success. Unfortunately, all of this tends to result in extra spending. Hands up: how many of you get a pay rise or a tax return and immediately know what you will spend it on? Assuming you haven't spent it before it even arrives.

Going back to Martin and Leah, I ended up spending the next hour or so sifting through their statements, trying desperately to find answers. As the hours went by, slowly I began finding what I believed were faults in the assistance that they had been given with their mortgages. I noticed in their desperation to stay afloat and keep their creditors happy they had been forced into making financial agreements that they couldn't possibly keep. Their creditors wanted their money back, but what was the point in asking them to make a weekly or fortnightly commitment that they just couldn't afford?

Of course, it would only be a matter of time before they failed yet again. It seemed pointless. I began calculating exactly how much money they had available and how much they needed each month. It was at this point that I realised that my program was relevant after all, even in their position. It's at this point that the option of a debt management company often creeps into a person's head. Let me assure you, if you take a few deep breaths and muster the strength, you can save yourself a lot of money by handling this on your own.

Together we went about telephoning every one of their creditors one by one. I had them authorise me to act as their representative and constructed affordable, reasonable offers to make to each of their creditors. Then I allocated their available funds accordingly to help them survive and stop the constant harassment calls hounding for money. Regardless of the plan, I knew they were still looking down the barrel of at least two more years of financial struggles as their court case progressed. Sitting at their big timber dining table that night, I could see their spirits slowly lifting as we worked through the list. This newly-devised money plan was giving them the breathing space that they so desperately needed.

Even with my mortgage broking background experience I knew I could not assist them with a refinance, as they were in default of their mortgage and were six months in arrears. Unfortunately, despite Leah now working, most lenders require six months good mortgage conduct and those that didn't were charging more than what they were paying already—a catch-22. What I did manage to do for them was renegotiate their existing mortgage. I could see from their loan statements and hardship history with their current lender that they had not received the best options or advice, despite their pleas for help. Lenders have a responsibility to offer an appropriate solution to a customer in hardship. This doesn't adequately account for a customer's personal situation or emotional stress. It merely serves to provide temporary relief and isn't necessarily the best option in the long term.

Allow me to explain. When Leah called her lender regarding her home loan, she was given the option of stopping her payments for three months. Although this seemed like a fabulous idea at the time, Leah's financial position was not likely to improve during that three-month period. After the initial three months, her lender expected the three months' payments to be repaid in full. On top of that, she was now also being charged penalty rates (usually set at 2% higher than her normal interest rate) and worse still, to keep her loan on track for the original 30-year term, her lender had readjusted her loan, which resulted in her monthly repayments now being at least $300 per month higher than they were prior to her reaching out for assistance.

Regrettably, prior to meeting with me she took this option twice, resulting in at least $10,000 being added to their loans. I proceeded to call her lender to try and move their loans from principle and interest to interest-only repayments. At the time, the interest rates were the same for both options, so they were not paying more interest for the privilege and they were totally aware of the consequences. This meant that they were not paying anything off the principle but, in exchange, it would reduce their monthly repayments by around $300 per month. Their compensation payout would ultimately deal with their loan in its entirety.

Please consider interest-only carefully—it's not usually the best solution. Given the poor choices previously offered, I was also able to have their all their penalty fees refunded and their interest rate lowered by 1% by connecting their loans to a package. Most annual package fees are around $395, but the package fee is accompanied by a discounted interest rate. In this case, the lower rate far outweighed the annual fee by a few thousand dollars per year. It wasn't much, but these simple adjustments resulted in an annual saving of around $5,000, in addition to the lesser monthly repayment—and that was just the beginning. I began to realise that I had provided a viable solution to their growing debt problem and could now justify the course workshop fee.

During my visit, I found myself taking a moment to relax. I found myself discreetly glancing over Leah's shoulder. I caught a glimpse of an array of beautiful statues proudly adorning their tall timber crystal cabinet, positioned oh-so-delicately against the dining room wall. Some of the statues where religious, others represented love, like a mother and baby statue. What struck me was the apparent need or want for an intervening spiritual power. I immediately sensed an expression of hope and faith.

At this point in the evening, the most important thing that I had offered them was hope—a renewed sense of *you can do it*. Strength and positivity is infectious. I believe it is also transferrable from one person to the next through goodwill, but only with a willing spirit. Whilst I could temporarily fix their situation and give them hope, it is was now their daily job to continue to nurture this hope with a willingness and strength to beat it. To win the game, so to speak. That's always the hardest part—to stay ahead of your opponent.

I took a gamble, not really knowing what their reactions would be, nor where the conversation would lead or even whether they would consider me to be over-stepping the mark, given that we had only met a few short hours earlier. "You look like you at least have your faith to keep you strong." I was totally shocked by their reply. "No, we gave up on that a long time ago." It deeply saddened me to hear that, especially with the strength that faith—or spiritually, as I prefer to call it—has provided me over the years, pulling me through some of my darkest days. They immediately insisted, as most do in their position, that God wasn't listening to their plight otherwise why would he allow this to happen to them?

"You just wouldn't understand how hard life is for us right now," they said. I suppose they never expected me to know first-hand just how hard their struggles really were. They were alone in their struggles, with the exception of their adult children who were offering financial assistance. They had also isolated themselves from extended family and friends who they felt were gloating at their perceived failure.

> *"I have total empathy for your position—I was where you are now, also completely through an unforeseen and unpredictable situation."*

I felt it was the right time to share my story, to show my compassion and understanding for their plight. "You don't really know how well I actually get what you are going through right now, but I do," I started. "I have total empathy for your position—I was where you are now, also completely through an unforeseen and unpredictable situation." I went back to the beginning.

It was a warm Melbourne morning around the beginning of December 2005. My crazy daily routine was about to get hectic in ways I could never have predicted. The kids loved to sleep in and were hard to get moving in the mornings—I dare say, nothing much has changed in that regard over the last 10 years. I finally managed to get everyone up, dressed and fed. Lunches all made, we began our daily ritual. Just getting out of the driveway was already much harder than seven years earlier when we had moved to our home. The roads were noticeably busier, so driving the short distance to the local primary school was a challenge, taking 15 minutes to drive just one kilometre.

We arrived at my son's primary school with only minutes to spare, having to make the mad dash from the car park across the school grounds and into his classroom. I went with him every day to get him settled, as he hated going to school. It was as if, in his mind, we were punishing him and didn't want him to have fun with us, so we sent him off to school. Far be it from the truth, but I could see his point; the girls were at home with me all day and he had to leave. It was a never-ending emotional struggle morning after morning that both he and I dreaded equally. The tears, the bargaining and begging me not to make him go; it was difficult for him, but for me it was particularly draining and brought back constant reminders of how I felt going to school each day.

I know I am the parent, but school issues bring a flood of bad memories. I don't cope well when it comes to bullying as I struggled with that myself. It's like it has the ability to switch on a light in my head that is almost blinding. I feel awful saying it but it was an emotional burden, wondering how he would cope at school during the day. I know I'm not alone. Watching your child suffering is any parents' nightmare. Thankfully, he eventually settled, and things began to improve. He had finally accepted his fate—that he would have to attend school every day for a very long time.

Next stop—my twin girls had to be dropped off at occasional care. Thank God, they absolutely loved going. It was the quite the opposite for them; they would get angry and upset with me if I said they weren't going that day. I had always been the type to look for better money solutions, so finding occasional care was the solution I needed to make working full time an affordable option. This was a much cheaper option for two three-year-olds at $10 per child per session than day care, which was $55 per child per day. It brought its own set of challenges: having to drop them off at 9am and pick them up by 12 noon, drop off at another centre offering a different time slot at 12.30pm, then head back to collect them by 3pm. Then it was time to race back to the primary school for a 3.15pm pickup and back home to drop all three kids off for my husband to take over from me after he finished work at 3pm.

This particular day turned out a little different to most. This time, after dropping the girls off, I rushed back to the real estate agency, where I had only just commenced employment a few months earlier. I walked in the door at approximately 9.05am. My husband and I had met the owner of the agency, Angus, 11 years earlier during the process of buying our first property as husband and wife through his company. Prior to me starting there, I had run into him on a few different occasions and we always got on very well. He is a real gentleman—the fatherly type—and we hit it off.

Every time we met he always asked me whether I was interested in pursuing a career in real estate. He said my bubbly personality and way with people would be a perfect fit. For years I resisted the temptation, despite my passion for the property market, which I had watched avidly since the age of 19. Now I felt differently. *Time for a change,* I thought. I accepted the offer and started working towards my Agents Representative Certificate at Victoria University in the evenings, so I could begin working as a real estate agent. I saw this as an opportunity for a long, exciting and rewarding new career for me, something that tied in nicely with my newly acquired mortgage broking and lending knowledge.

As I sat at my desk that morning, nothing could have prepared me for the events that would follow. It almost seems impromptu that the newspaper was positioned at the end of my desk. Typically, I would not look at the paper except to flip the pages and read the real estate section. Somehow, that day the front-page headline just jumped out and caught my eye. It read something along the lines of "ASIC freezes company" which I read with intrigue.

First came that awful wave, that horrid sick feeling. You know, the one that you get when your heart suddenly sinks into the pit of your stomach, followed by a tightening sensation of the chest muscles, and a shortness of breath. Then the trembling hands as a rush of adrenaline and the overwhelming sense of stress and anxiety passes through your entire body. I sat speechless and daunted at my desk. I had to get away quickly, to remove myself from the sight of others. I moved swiftly from my desk trying desperately to avoid eye contact as I was now fighting desperately to hold back the tears. I feared the embarrassment of bursting into tears in front of my work colleagues—how unprofessional I would appear. I had almost successfully made it as far as the toilets, which were located at the rear of the offices, thinking nobody had noticed.

My colleagues knew me well. One of my fellow co-workers, Anna, had obviously sensed my distraught behaviour, noticing my actions were out of character and ran in behind me. "What's wrong, are you okay?" she asked. I could hardly speak, my voice was crackling, and my heart was now pounding out of chest. My head was spinning at a million miles per hour. I felt nauseous and faint.

We had signed a contract in June with a long settlement period. All those months earlier, we had expressed our interest in a property to the vendor's agent, but insisted that our money was tied up and would not be returned to us until December 31st, 2005; if we were to agree and sign a contract of sale, it would need to have a long, seven-month settlement period. She had consulted with the vendors and they were happy with the timeframe, so we set the settlement date for January 10th, 2006.

> *"They can take everything away from me, but the one thing they can't and won't take is my smile."*

This date would not only comfortably coincide with the repayment of our investment funds, but also give us a small window of time in case of any unforeseen delays, and provide us with enough time to undertake some minor renovations in our current home.

As I stood there trying to compose myself, it became apparent that our money would not be returned to us. It was only three weeks before Christmas and, despite all my attempts at being so well-organised, suddenly we had no money and the awful prospect of facing bankruptcy seemed all too real. I couldn't help but think, *how could this be happening to us?* How could we go from financially comfortable to financially destitute, all overnight?

As I stood, barely able to support my body from collapsing on the floor, the office manager approached me. I don't know how she thought it would be of comfort to me, but she said, "Gosh Belinda, you must have run over a Chinese man and a black cat at the same time. If I were you I'd jump off the Westgate Bridge." For those of you who don't know, this was the highest bridge in Melbourne at the time. I looked at her in complete and utter astonishment—*did she actually just say that*? Looking back now, it's quite funny.

Luckily for me, I had a different attitude. I was a mother of three children under seven, for goodness sake. I said, then and there, "They can take everything away from me, but the one thing they can't and won't take is my smile." In my desperate attempt to stay focused, I told myself that this would not bring us down. There would be a way forward and if there was one person in this world that could find it, it was me. I was admired for my strength and positive attitude. I would later prove that it serves me well.

Seven years earlier, in 1997, we had purchased our family home in the quaint bayside suburb of Williamstown in Victoria, Australia. It was a well-maintained, sturdy 1920s Californian bungalow. Unlike most of the similar period style homes in the surrounding area, it was in pretty good condition, especially given its age. Better still, it was on a relatively large block of land—approximately 820 square metres. Perfect for raising a young family, we thought. It was also close to the Melbourne CBD and considered to be a trendy, up-and-coming beach suburb.

Typically, my husband never looked at the local newspaper let alone the real estate section, but this day he saw an editorial. The house ticked all our boxes. I told him he should ring the agent, as it was him who found the property. He came back to me with a disappointed look on his face and said the agent had told him it was going to be sold that night. He had received an offer that the vendors were happy with and so, unlike me, my husband said, "Thank you and goodbye."

I looked at him with astonishment, shaking my head. I said, "But if we offer more, surely they will sell it to us instead." He was embarrassed; no way was he going to call back and suggest such a thing—I had to make the call. "Okay, you have exactly 30 minutes to meet me at the house or it will be sold to the other people," the agent said. We literally ran to the car, knowing it would take that long to drive there. The agent was patiently waiting outside. He opened the door and we proceeded to walk through the house. By this stage we had seen so many houses that we simply walked down the hallway which ran from front to back, stepped outside into the backyard, then quickly turned around and walked straight back out the front door. The agent began to casually stroll down the driveway back towards the street—he probably thought we were another pair of time wasters.

I politely yelled to get his attention as he had his back towards us. "Excuse me!" He turned and walked back towards us. "We'll take it—how much?" I don't think I will ever see such a priceless reaction ever again. He nearly fell over. Looking back, he probably thought it was the easiest commission he had ever made in his career. A five-second inspection and he had sold us a house. "$195,000," he said.

"But I will need a 10% deposit right now." I think he still thought we were messing with him. I reached into my bag, pulled out our cheque book and without so much as a moment's hesitation, I wrote him a cheque for $19,500. That would have to be one of the happiest cheques we have ever written. We were in the exquisitely fine position of having the ability to confidently write a cheque. We were so excited to have finally found our *almost* dream property.

Unlike most people our age (I was 31 and my husband was 38) we were then already in a comfy financial position where we were able to pay the whole $195,000 in cash. We didn't win the lottery, nor did we inherit money. We had saved the whole lot, something that most could never afford to do, at least not on the average wages that we both had. Life was admittedly looking pretty good. Only a couple of weeks after the settlement took place, we would lock the house up and embark on a two-month vacation to Europe that we had booked after giving up our search for a new home.

Years later, we were enjoying regular overseas family holidays and all the mod-cons you could think of, including three brand new cars. A little selfish, I know—there were only two of us, so why did we need three cars? My husband had worked and saved hard, so the time seemed right for him to have that well-earned, beautiful sports car he had always wanted. He wanted to buy a Ferrari but it only had two seats. At that time we were already a family of three and wanting a second child, so it seemed stupid for him to buy a two-seater, as he rarely went out on his own. I convinced him—wrongly, in hindsight—not to spend so much and save the rest. Hindsight is a wonderful thing, as you will see later. We all know cars are a depreciating asset. Sometimes you need to spoil yourself a little—but only if you can afford to lose the money, right?

I had not planned on returning to work while the kids were still small, but it seemed unavoidable. If we wanted to upgrade and live in a slightly better location, we needed to earn more. We always knew that paying a mortgage would be challenging on one wage, which is why we worked so hard to pay off our first house. Now we knew that it was time for me to look at taking on work if we were taking on another mortgage, albeit a relatively small one. We had discovered the harsh reality that, even without a mortgage or any other debts, on one income it just wasn't possible to save much. Sure, we had enough for our annual overseas trips at around $8,000 a year, but as far as the bank was concerned, it was not enough to qualify for a mortgage. I made the decision to return to work—it made sense. Initially, I looked for part-time work at night-time while the kids were sleeping, but the work was so monotonous. I decided to start my own business as a mortgage broker so that I could work from home and still be with the kids during the day. It also offered more flexible working hours. It seemed a natural progression; I knew and understood loans and how to operate them—it was a perfect fit for me.

We had never really planned to buy that almost-perfect house in North Williamstown. We preferred the south end, but we had spent years scouring the suburbs without success. The perfect house for us needed a side driveway, a side-by-side double garage, four bedrooms and a large yard. So, when we finally found something that matched perfectly with all our wants, it just happened to be on the other side. We loved our current home, but it was always our intention to sell and move to South Williamstown at some point. It was the quainter side of the suburb, closer to the beach. We were on the main thoroughfare in our current home, whereas the streets on the other side were cosy.

Years later, in June 2005, I drove down one of my favourite streets saw a wreck of a house. You know the kind—the worst house on the best street. It fit that bill perfectly. I parked in front of the "for sale" board and noticed that the auction date was coming up, but it was to be while we were away in Vanuatu on a family vacation. Somehow, I got caught up in all the excitement of going on holiday and I completely forgot about the auction. Two weeks later, after arriving home, I remembered seeing the house and I drove by to see if it had sold. To my surprise, it was still available. I believed this was a sign saying that it was meant for us. I immediately called the agent and asked if there had been any offers—she said no. I called my husband, told him it was still up for sale and that we should go and look at it before it gets snapped up.

That afternoon, we went down, did an inspection and promptly entered negotiations to buy the property. Astoundingly, the agent suddenly had another interested party. "*Really?*" we thought. We hoped that we were not being conned into paying more and cleverly asked to do a round table auction, so we could see if there really was another interested party. It seemed like our only chance. We set ourselves a bidding cap, as you do, but secretly I just had to have it. Frank was happy to settle anywhere, but happily supported the decision. Just like me, he loved our current home but had always wanted to relocate to the south of the suburb. We couldn't know if there would be another opportunity for us to be able to afford to buy into this street again.

Typically, houses in this street were going for a million-plus. Just a few doors up, I had recently gone to an auction and the property sold for $1.1 million. Six years earlier, we had fallen in love with a beautiful two-storey house, which just so happened to be opposite this house. Much to our disappointment, it had sold for $730,000, which was far more than we could afford back then. I was without a job and at that point I was still thinking I wanted to be a stay-at-home mum forever. The time was now, and we had to act quickly.

For us, it felt like perfect timing. We could secure a home in a street we both liked, and we only needed to borrow about $200,000 after selling our house. This would allow us to buy and renovate it into a lovely home that would be worth more than $1 million on completion. My husband did question whether we could afford such a debt. It seemed like a lot of money at the time, but I assured him that I was prepared to work full-time again, which is why I took on the job at the real estate agency. I had already set up the mortgage business the year prior but with three kids under six, working on commission, I needed a more regular income. I thought taking on the real estate job would enable me to have that ongoing regular wage. So, in June 2005 we signed the contract of sale to buy this run-down house. Finally, our dreams were all coming together. The house was $780,000 and with government stamp duty we would need $830,000. The plan was that we would sell our house for around $700,000 and borrow the remainder with enough to do a simple renovation.

Going back to that awful December morning, after I read that newspaper article I knew we were in big trouble and our dreams seemed to shatter instantly. After composing myself enough to speak, I picked up the phone and began calling real estate agents, one after the other, asking that they instantly put our investment properties up for sale. We had two weeks before the banks would close for Christmas and a few days into the new year to raise $830,000. We had our loan approval in place already so that we could buy the old house without needing to sell our home, but the approval was only for $470,000. We had planned to add our returned investment funds of $360,000, but suddenly we needed the whole amount, as we weren't going to see any of our money back in time for the settlement. I was trying to keep it all together, not just for me but for Frank and the kids. I knew somehow, I had to stay strong. Frank was at work and I didn't want to tell him what I had discovered for fear of something happening to him at work, so I decided to keep it a secret until I arrived home that night.

I did, however, make one stop on the way home that night and that was to the medical clinic. I had experienced chest pains all day and thought I could be having a heart attack. I lay on the bed while they connected all the ECG points and waited for the bad news. "Belinda, it's okay, you are not having a heart attack," the doctor told me. "I think what you are suffering from is a panic attack." I had heard about them but didn't know what they felt like first-hand. This would be the first of many panic attacks that I would suffer from over the coming years. Here I was, working a full day, on a basic retainer, earning what I thought was peanuts. I was trying desperately to sell houses, now with all this added stress, so much I could barely stand, hardly breathe. Holding back tears was a challenge. I can still remember those feelings so well. It felt as though someone had their foot on my chest, crushing it. I was short of breath and the tears kept coming. I tried desperately to hold myself together but it was hard. I had no choice—I had to maintain my sanity.

Thankfully, I was good with planning and, with only three weeks until Christmas, I had already bought most of the kids' presents. I liked to pick them up throughout the year, which saved us that year. Food, on the other hand—that was another story. We lived across the road from Safeway and I remember saying to my husband, "I'm just going to run across the road and grab some milk." I returned empty-handed. Looking at the price tag on the shelf I felt like I was going to burst into tears, so I had to leave. Stupid, I know, but this was the first of many stressful and tearful days that would follow.

Upon realising that we would struggle to settle the property, given the impending settlement date, I had to come up with solutions quickly. I contacted our conveyancer and explained our situation. Liz was great—she agreed that, to avoid us incurring extra legal costs, I could construct my own letters for her to send on our behalf to the vendor's solicitors. My years of working in a legal practice were finally coming in handy—but the response was not so good. They basically advised us that they would take us down and show no mercy. All I could see was the potential for costs to escalate to a huge payout bill.

I went into instant protection mode, like a mother bear protecting her cubs. I needed to salvage whatever money we could to avoid having to declare bankruptcy. At the time, I thought we had no option but to try and appeal, show the vendors we were genuine people; a young family who accidentally got caught out. We decided to approach the owners directly in the hope that they could extend the settlement date or possibly consider vendor finance. We didn't know whether they had already bought somewhere else, but this would hopefully give us some extra breathing space. With three small kids in tow we swallowed our pride and gently knocked on their front door, cringing in anticipation. It was our only chance, we had to try and explain our situation, but more so, it was an attempt to also reassure them that we still wanted to buy the house. We just needed some extra time to raise the extra funds, given our position.

Standing on the doorstep waiting for them to come to the door seemed like a lifetime. My emotions were running high. Looking back now, I don't know how we managed to stand there so calmly. Finally, they answered the door and with a blank, almost heartless glance, without even flinching, they looked at us and said, "If you don't leave now we will call the police." We could hardly believe our ears. Our hearts felt like they had been stampeded by a thousand elephants—we were crushed. I can't even contemplate how my husband was feeling. It must have killed him inside, particularly as it was my dumb idea. I had yet again convinced him that people aren't all bad and that we should try. That we had nothing to lose; we could only gain, particularly at this point in the game.

And so, with our tails between our legs, we left the property, devastated and feeling helpless. They wouldn't listen, not even for a moment, to anything we had to say, let alone give us time to plead our case and resolve the problem. Instead, they were heartless and felt no compassion towards us. They owed us nothing, I know that, but to not even have showed us a little respect for the difficulties we were facing—maybe I expected too much. On the other hand, maybe they were trying to remain tough. I suppose it was also causing them stress. Perhaps their dream to move had also been crushed by us. Maybe they saw us as selfish—I guess I will never know the answer.

The reality stood strong for us. Their solicitors had written to us, advising that, on their clients' instructions, they wished to convey the harsh reality that if we didn't proceed with the settlement, not only would they sue us for the agent's selling commission—some $16,000—but they would also seek costs for re-advertising and all fees associated with the resale of the property along, with any resale shortfall. It quickly became apparent that any money we might have left over after selling everything would evaporate into thin air, eaten up with what I deemed to be unnecessary legal costs, commissions and the like. We simply could not let that happen. That option seemed limitless. What if they resold the house for next to nothing? Everything we had would be gone forever.

It seemed like we only had one option. We would need to raise the necessary funds, if only to settle the house on time so that we could relist it for sale again ourselves. At least that way we would be in control of the outcome. We couldn't risk losing even more money—there had to be a way out.

With the banks starting to wind down for Christmas and only 12 business days left, we embarked on the unenviable task of liquidating our assets as a priority. With no time to spare for emotions we began raising the money we were short for the settlement—we needed $830,000. We increased the proposed mortgage to $624,000, which also came at a hefty price, as we would now also need to pay the Lenders mortgage insurance in the interim. We set out to sell anything we could as quickly as possible. That was the heart-breaking moment when treasured baby toys became worth more than their sentimental value.

Then my phone rang. I don't typically answer calls from unknown numbers, but this time I did. At first, I was puzzled, pondering who I was speaking with—then I made the association. The woman introduced herself as Karen. She lived on a property just up the road from our holiday property, a gorgeous 20-acre country farmlet outside the town of Ballarat in the Victorian Goldfields. We had found it after a long, hard search (remember the Jersey cows we encountered on our search?) in 2003 and used our savings to pay cash—$56,000, to be precise. We also bought an old 26-foot Franklin caravan from a dealer in Yan Yean, hired a four-wheel-drive and towed it two-and-a-half hours to our property. We'd spent a few months renovating the interior so that it looked sparklingly new. It accommodated our family of five comfortably, with two sets of bunk beds (which gave us a spare bed in case the kids wanted to invite a friend to stay) and a double, together with a kitchenette, a new dining table and upholstered couches.

We had carefully positioned it on our land to take full advantage of the view of the rolling green hills, the picture of tranquillity and peace. We planned to build and possibly retire on the property. Karen told me that our adjacent neighbour, Geraldine, had passed on our details to her. She began by asking us if she could put her horses on our farm as she had no feed left, whereas our grass was high and our dams still had a little water. Of course we obliged—after all, isn't that what fellow country neighbours do for each other? She had appealed to our good nature and began to befriend me. She expressed how Geraldine had informed her that she and I had a common factor—we both had a set of twins.

As the discussion progressed I discovered that not only was she raising a set of twins, then under the age of one, but that she and her husband were raising a total of seven young children, including a daughter with severe disabilities. She went on to tell me that years earlier, while pregnant, she was involved in a car accident which resulted in her daughter not only being born premature but with cerebral palsy. This particularly struck a chord for us, as my husband's brother Sam was also wheelchair-bound, living with cerebral palsy. Our compassion and sympathy for their daily life struggles made our story suddenly feel insignificant.

She had successfully dropped my guard and somehow managed to gain my trust; despite all my current anxieties, she had successfully tugged on my emotions. She then proceeded to direct the conversation in such a way that Geraldine had told her that I might have baby clothes or the like that I wanted to part with. I said we had found ourselves in a difficult situation and that her timing was impeccable, that we were moving very soon and we desperately needed to sell off unneeded items to raise funds for our impending settlement. I asked her if she was interested, as I had a whole array of beautiful, expensive baby toys, all of which were as new as the day I had bought them. I had reluctantly planned to list and sell them on eBay, so if she was interested in looking at them I would consider selling them to her and would hold off advertising them.

She arranged a time and made the two-hour drive to our home in Melbourne. She arrived around lunchtime and carefully took her time, continuing to ask if we had anything else we wanted to sell. She continued to meander through our garage where we had stored everything to declutter the house in preparation for our impending auction, due a week or so later. They chose things to take home with them. They knew of our plight. All we could see at that moment was a blessing. I tend to always believe that everything happens for a reason, so it made good sense—God had sent these people to us. We were so grateful that we could all benefit from our distressing situation, a win/win for everyone. One by one, they hand-loaded our precious memories into their big, glossy-black, fully-enclosed trailer that they towed so proudly behind their new people-mover. They had told us that the insurance company had given it to them. Don't get me wrong; despite everything, I would never have wanted to trade lives with them, not even for a day. As much as our suffering seemed, theirs was harder and it was forever. I knew ours was only temporary and for that I am eternally grateful.

I had wanted to put all those fabulous baby toys in a keepsake box for when our grandchildren arrived a couple of decades later, but given our current position, I had no choice but to part with them. These toys held so many memories, but I had to replace my sadness with the relief that we would get some of the money we needed to settle. After loading up our treasured possessions— they took a lot, including some oil paintings—Karen turned to me, explained that she did not have the cash with her and asked if she could pay us in fortnightly instalments, handing me a $100 gesture. At that particular moment we hesitated, taken aback by what had just occurred. I think we were in complete shock but felt we had little option but to agree. We made a gentleman's agreement and wished them a safe trip home. In good faith, we let Karen and her husband drive off.

In hindsight, they probably high-fived each other on yet another successful scam. We waited patiently, checking our account regularly, but the payments never came. Finally, we decided to drive to Ballarat and pay them a visit. I had the unenviable task of going to her door. I knocked and waited patiently. At first, she pretended not to be home, but we could hear and see them inside. Then finally she opened the door. I politely asked her for the money she owed us, or to return the goods she took. Without so much as a blink of her eye she confidently said, "I don't have them. I dropped them at the op shop—it was all rubbish." "What?" I said, in complete and utter astonishment at what she had just said. "That's nonsense and you know it. You must have sold them on eBay." I said. She proceeded to say, "I can't pay you. My husband and I broke up and now I'm trying to raise the kids by myself." I offered my sympathies, but continued, "That has nothing to do with the fact that you took my things. If you can't pay me that's fine—just give them back to me."

She insisted that they were worthless rubbish and then added further insult. "I told you, I am a single mother—my husband left me!" I shook my head; I couldn't believe what I was hearing. I looked at her in disgust and anger. For the first time in my life, I felt like I might need to be restrained. I wanted to strangle her on the spot. With tears streaming down my face and disbelief turning into dismay, I said, "Whether that's true or not, it is irrelevant—just give me my things back." She closed the door in my face. I turned and walked back to the car as Frank and the kids looked at me, wondering what had transposed during the conversation.

We left. As we drove up the road, we spotted the people mover parked in the gravel with her husband sitting behind the wheel. It all made sense. She had obviously called him upon seeing us drive into her property and told him not to return until we had gone. Never in my life have I experienced such hatred and disgust, and wanted to hurt someone as much as I did at that very moment. We left empty-handed and made the long journey back home again. I can't remember whether we asked her to remove her horses from our property at that point, but I surely hope we did.

We couldn't help but continue to question ourselves daily. Could it be that she had planned all along to scam us? At that point I think both of us began to wonder whether all the things people had said about us were true. Were we gullible? Stupid? Greedy? You can't even imagine the feelings of anguish, the doubts that flooded through my brain, desperately trying not to believe that anyone could be so callous, manipulative and deceitful. Looking back, it's easy to see that they probably had such a nice trailer because they were professional scammers; disgusting people, using their personal tragedy to abuse and deceive innocent families everywhere. Never had my emotions turned to the ugly side like that. We both found ourselves feeling resentful, but being who we were, this now meant that we were suffering the emotional consequences of our ill thoughts and feeling worse for having them. Unbelievably, we weren't even capable of wishing these awful people harm without it eating away at us.

For the first time in our lives, at a time when we needed money so desperately, things just didn't seem to be going in our favour. Secretly, I was crumbling inside but on the outside, I put up a strong front. I had to remain focused and continue to believe that it would all somehow still work out alright. With our existing home now ready for auction, looking bright and wonderful, with an improved bathroom, which now had a new spa bath, and a freshly painted kitchen with modern

At that point I think both of us began to wonder whether all the things people had said about us were true. Were we gullible? Stupid? Greedy?

cupboard doors, a pantry and all new appliances, we patiently awaited the crowds on auction day—but nobody came. It was a complete disaster. We now had no offers to even consider. Sure, it was a main road but it was an absolutely perfect family home with facilities that most in Williamstown lacked. It had a large block, a long side driveway that lead to a double garage, four bedrooms and it was rock solid, unlike most homes in the area that cracked with movement. It left us questioning everything; should we have saved our money not renovated and sold for less? You name it, we were thinking it.

We had now reached the point when reality had sunk in. When you have exhausted all avenues and you are left with no alternative but to beg for help. I would never wish for anyone to experience what we went through. I think begging evokes a real sense of fear which triggers anger within yourself. We had hit rock bottom. There didn't seem to be anything lower than where we were now. For my husband, it was a loss of pride and a sense of failure. Those feelings of shame and embarrassment still linger on, even a decade later. The sheer humiliation of going from self-sufficient to starvation, almost overnight, and now having to beg for help, was horrendous. Our situation was undeniable; we simply could not do it on our own. We had drained all our resources and it took every ounce of strength we had to muster up the courage to ask for help.

What we didn't anticipate was that, by opening up and exposing our plight, we would further subject ourselves to the ridicule and judgement of others. These were people we trusted, that we thought loved us unconditionally, but not so. They added to our hurt, shame and anguish with an explosion of unseen criticism. Was it any wonder Leah and Martin had played it safe, instead choosing to share their secret anguish with only a select few? We noticed that suddenly, everyone was an expert. "How could you have been so selfish?" "Obviously, you were consumed by greed." "Why were you so stupid?" The list was endless. Talk about punishment. Losing the money wasn't even the hardest part of this tragic event. The harsh reality was that we were experiencing a sense of loss, grieving for our financial

> *We had hit rock bottom. There didn't seem to be anything lower than where we were now.*

independence, but also our faith in humanity. It was a betrayal, not just by strangers, which in retrospect was nothing compared with having to swallow the criticism and endure what felt like endless torture from those who supposedly cared about us the most.

I suppose as humans we should know never to expect anything from people, especially those you don't know and it's certainly true what they say—*money changes everything*. Reactions are often surprising, but what we didn't count on was people being so brutal. In their eyes, because we were reaching out for help, they suddenly had the right to judge us. It was almost as if we were criminals and they were the jury. Right from the onset, we were assumed to be the guilty party, the stupid, greedy ones. We had to prove our innocence—but why should we?

My efforts were fruitless. In hindsight, I can see that I too was caught up in my own story, resulting in me wasting far too much energy trying to justify the behaviours of others, or why we had done what we did. I have always lived my life and taught my children, "Do unto others as you would have done to you." To this day that remains unchanged. I am responsible for myself and my actions. Sure, we probably made poor decisions and trusted the wrong people, but we have to live with that and, most importantly, we will never make the same mistakes again. However, what I refuse to accept is that those same decisions would have been made by us had we been told the real facts about our investment. We would never have risked anything intentionally. I had to force myself to focus on the real facts. We had not come this far in life financially through being frivolous, let alone stupid or greedy.

We have never gambled—quite the contrary. We had once gone on one of those pokies weekends in New South Wales because friends had asked us to come along. Even then we struggled to part with a dollar coin, instead preferring not to risk losing it. We weren't the kind of family to throw good money after bad, probably because we knew the odds were stacked against us. We have only ever had the occasional social drink, we don't smoke and we had no pets, until recently when our 16-year-old daughter agreed to pay for all the expenses for her dog. Yet, we were classed as greedy. We had no choice; we needed help and in exchange we had to suck it up and listen. We took full responsibility for our decisions. It was such a difficult time, as I tried so desperately to console the family and rectify the situation the best way I knew how. It certainly taught us an expensive lesson, one that still holds strong for us, even today. We learned never to trust anyone with our money again and to go back to what had been so successful for us in the past. Empowering yourself with knowledge is a vital element of success, so that you have the skillset to make good decisions.

Desperate times call for desperate measures. At this point, it wouldn't be fair on you to claim that I was a complete picture of strength. I was like a ball bouncing all over the place; my stress levels were at an all-time high and at times I was emotionally erratic, even yelling at the kids. I wasn't abusive and didn't hurt them physically. I still had boundaries that I never crossed, but I was slowly losing my patience over silly, insignificant things. I would trip on a toy and hurt myself and then get angry that they had not put it away. I felt like I was out of control and, although I was extremely focused on the money task before me, the simple things were getting harder, like food shopping and cooking. I became disorganised; mind you, I would never claim to be good at either of those things at the best of times. I haven't ever had the luxury of just relaxing at home and being a mum, because I have always challenged myself to reach beyond my scope or capacity. There were moments when, for a split second, I thought in my mind that if I died my family would have my life insurance and that would fix all our financial problems. These thoughts occurred more than once, I think as a reflex reaction to the stress I was under. I remembered during my evening visit with Martin, he too had suggested that he was worth more dead than alive.

> *Suicide is all too often a very real option but it is definitely avoidable.*

Suicide is all too often a very real option but it is definitely avoidable. I would say I was depressed at times, but with good reason—there simply wasn't enough money to go around. I also became acutely aware of my deficiencies and could feel and recognise the symptoms as they changed. Having seen customers that suffered from clinical depression, I was able to see the difference. They were unaware or unable to stop themselves from slipping further, whereas I was always conscious of my feelings and was still able to stop them dead in their tracks. Depression and stress were like a fine line in the sand—a line I skipped over time and time again. At times, I was completely exhausted and my mind was so muddled I became extremely forgetful, not with the big ticket items, more with the routine things in life. I found that I was able to care for the kids but not myself. I always put myself last on the list. I noticed that I was jumbling my words and forgetting simple things like where I parked the car. Things that I once took for granted seemed to slip through the cracks.

I felt alone and sought solitude, not just because I wasn't coping but because I felt I couldn't talk to anyone. Crying seemed to be a daily ritual. I often felt like a champagne bottle that had been shook up and was spilling over. I think when you are consumed with fear and guilt—and by that I mean believing that you should have known better or made different decisions—your thinking is obscured and logic is thrown aside. Occasionally, dying felt like a solution, an instant fix to the problem. Sometimes it felt like a good option but then I felt weak for thinking that way. Thankfully, logic took over and the prospect of my children growing up without their mother overrode any thought or temptation to consider such a ludicrous solution. Along with the love I have for them, the excitement of being a grandparent one day is something I hold dear. Sadly, I can understand why so many people feel it's the only remedy, as wrong as it may be.

In times of vulnerability and asking for help, regretfully you may be at the mercy of others. Those you know, love and trust may take the opportunity to kick you while you're down, adding insult to your already exposed injuries. People sometimes feel the need to assess your financial worthiness and may deem you unworthy or a risk. I don't think they have any concept of the hurt you experience when hearing this—that they may just destroy what little self-respect you have left. It hurts; it's like cutting you open and pouring salt into your already bleeding wounds rather than offering you bandages and comfort. You may even wonder if you would be so harsh if the shoe was on the other foot.

Fortunately for us, not everyone was the same. I called my brother Warren, in sheer and utter desperation. Trying to compose myself, I explained to him that something terrible had happened. Something we could never have anticipated, especially with less than four weeks of our investment left. I was broken and, despite being at the other end of the telephone, I knew he felt my pain, despite my attempts to hide my anguish. He consoled me; I could sense he truly understood. He offered to do what he could to help us. I explained to him that we would repay him every cent and pay whatever interest he incurred—we just needed enough time to sell off all our assets. I asked him if he wanted to see our financials. "No!" he replied, in a very assertive manner. "Don't be ridiculous, you are my sister. If you tell me you can repay us, I trust you." I was speechless; the lump in my throat was so big I could barely swallow. I was so humbled by his compassion and willingness to help, without judgement or an ill word to speak of. I continued to reassure him that we could definitely raise the funds required to repay him. Even if it meant we sold at a rock bottom price, he would see every cent back. He told me that he could not make the decision alone and that he would first need to speak to his wife, Joanne.

I can only imagine how hard it was for them that night. I think the overriding factor for them was that they were in a position to help save not only us, but their nieces and nephew as well. I can't begin

It's not always about money—some people don't have it to give.

to express how very blessed we felt that my only brother wanted to help us, and that his wife too felt our pain and couldn't bear to see us lose everything. Thank God we have them in our lives. They went the very next day to their bank, increased the mortgage on their own home by as much as they could and gave us a cheque for $100,000. We were now getting closer to the target with almost all the money we were short. Thankfully we were also blessed with wonderful parents who gave us $70,000. They too wanted to do whatever they could to help us. We were now at $800,000 and getting closer to meeting the deadline. It's not always about money—some people don't have it to give. My mother gave us moral support and helped by looking after the children and cooking meals, which was invaluable. Without these five amazing people, I don't know how we could have pulled it off—we are forever grateful to have them in our lives.

We were only $32,000 short of the settlement funds we needed with a few days to go. Keeping in mind that without the extra $32,000 there wasn't going to be a settlement. My husband had a beautiful silver Saab Aero convertible he had bought in 2000 for $94,000. He had wanted a Ferrari or a Mercedes, but that would have meant spending extra and, worse still, a two-year wait. Stupidly, I had convinced him to spend the $20,000 less and buy the Saab. Although it was a fantastic car it depreciated—like most cars, only a little faster. We had paid cash and it was in immaculate condition, having only travelled 8,000 kilometres. I called around to see if anyone wanted to buy the car. A previous client of mine called back and told me he knew a guy at an auction company based in South Melbourne who was interested in purchasing the car.

My husband jumped into the Saab and I followed behind in my car with the kids. We drove it down to South Melbourne with the intention of not returning home with it that afternoon. We had been told he would pay us $36,000. However, once again we would be disappointed. "Oh, it's a 2000 model," he began. "I thought it was 2001. Sorry, I can only give you $30,000 for it." As if we weren't destroyed enough parting with it for $36,000, now it was $6,000 less. "No way, they aren't getting my car for that," my husband said. "I don't care how much we are short." So, we drove home. Sometimes in life you just need to stand up for what's right. Even though at that moment I felt desperate, I supported the decision, believing again that there must be a good reason for this happening.

On the way home we passed a local spot where people typically parked cars on the main road that they were trying to sell. With only days to go, we decided we too would park the car there and hopefully it would sell quickly, in time for settlement day. Unfortunately, about 30 minutes after leaving the car there we received a call from a person saying, "If I were you, I would move your car—you will get a ticket for parking it there." I suppose we will never know whether it was a disgruntled neighbour sick of cars constantly parking in front of their house or if it was someone who genuinely was looking out for us. I prefer to believe it was the latter. Regardless, the last thing we needed in a time of financial crisis was to add a fine to our already growing financial stress, so we thanked them, returned to pick up the car and drove it back to our house. As we arrived home, knowing we had no options left, I said, "Why don't you just park it in front of our house and see how we go? You never know." Our house was on a main road and saw a lot of traffic—what did we have to lose?

My faith has always remained strong. I prayed that the car would sell and about an hour later my husband's mobile phone rang. There was a gentleman outside standing next to the car—he wanted to inspect it. We peeked cautiously through the curtains, trying to make sure he didn't see us. He had pulled up and was driving an identical car to ours. Even the colour was the same, so we wondered what was going on. We went outside and met him. He explained that he was given the car he was driving on loan from the car yard for a week to test drive it and that he loved it so much that he had decided to buy it, but thought he should wash it before returning it to the yard. He had taken the car to a car wash near his house but it was really busy and he needed to hurry back to the yard before it closed. He asked around and someone told him that there was another carwash along the other main road. That road just happened to be the main road that we lived on, where he spotted our "for sale" sign—a real miracle if you ask me. There simply isn't any other way to explain that chain of events. God was truly manipulating the situation to bring the two of us together.

We were only days from settlement, short by only $32,000 and he offered to pay us the $36,000 we so desperately needed. Of course, he wanted to know why we would sell the car with only 8,000 kilometres on it, and so I explained our plight. "Don't worry," he said. "I can give you cash on Monday, so you don't need to wait for the funds to clear for your settlement." Our prayers had been answered. Now we were able to settle the property, without even needing an extension.

We immediately called our conveyancer Liz, who shared our sense of absolute relief and the pleasure of knowing that we had managed to achieve our goal. She had the luxury of advising the vendor's solicitor that we were ready to settle. I called the real estate agent to arrange the final inspection on the Friday. This time, waiting in the car outside the property was quite a different experience; a rather bittersweet moment, in fact, at a time in our lives where potential disaster intersected with a future filled with opportunity. The agent thought she knew us well, yet she was oblivious to our desperation to settle on time. Together, we walked towards the front door. She put the key in the lock and delicately opened the front door. You could certainly feel her willingness to shed happiness throughout the house as she welcomed us into what she believed would be our new home and new beginning. On the other hand, we entered cautiously—all we now saw before our eyes was a huge money pit.

Glancing from side to side, searching for any positives, I couldn't help but be drawn back to what had previously been the master bedroom. All I could see was the plaster in the front bedroom, barely hanging onto the ceiling. It looked as though one swift shake of the house would bring it all down onto your bed, crushing you as you slept. I stood motionless, fearing the thought of what a large truck driving by could do to the home. The entrance hall was a very different story. Whilst it didn't pose the same threat to our

God was truly manipulating the situation to bring the two of us together.

lives, it too felt like a health risk. It had dried dog's slobber up the walls—that's what we thought it was, anyway. Although the guilty golden retriever wasn't standing before us, you could still see its remnants stuck to the surrounding walls, skirting boards and even the floorboards. We could see the door handles and their surrounds were black with filth, as though a motor mechanic coming home after a hard day's work had rubbed his hands all over the doors and around the light switches.

Moving through to the kitchen, it was evident that they had tried to remove the vinyl from the beautiful wide Baltic timber floorboards, perhaps hoping to polish them to make the house look nicer. At this point, I couldn't possibly call it a home. Obviously, things hadn't quite gone to plan as the vinyl was half-on, half-off. They had obviously started, but not finished its removal, as it was securely fastened with glue to the floor. Rather than put some extra elbow grease into removing it, they instead chose to abandon the task. The dog had clearly taken the opportunity to relax on the area with the missing pieces, leaving traces of its long golden hairs stuck fastly in the remaining hardened glue. There was a crappy extension added to the rear of the home with a ceiling and roof that slants downwards, as opposed to the lovely, 10-foot high ceiling throughout the rest of the house. It was barely high enough for me to walk through. There was a shower; I couldn't begin to explain how disgusting and dirty it was—certainly not fit for a human.

I wish I had taken pictures, because words cannot accurately describe what I saw. This area was clearly the doghouse because it stank so badly I couldn't bear to go in there. Walking through the home, it was hard to conceive that someone could have been living here in this state, particularly with young children. It was so repulsive and filthy—a poor reflection on those heartless individuals that had greeted us a few weeks before.

Once again, my heart was pounding. As I moved from room to room in utter disgust, I will never forget the agent's face as she looked at me, not knowing what was happening to us and said in a cheery tone, "Well, is it just as you remember?" I tried so desperately to hold back the tears and put on a brave face, but all I could muster was, "No, I can't believe that we actually bought this disgusting piece of crap." The expression on her face was priceless.

Just six months earlier we had visited the exact same house, with complete optimism and excitement. My mother had always had a vision for design and colour. I never understood it when I was younger but now, in my late thirties, I had it too. I had the ability to look at the old and visualise the new. It had so much potential—glistening chandeliers and period-style attributes that befitted the home so nicely—and yet now all I could see was the filth. Perception is reality. It was the same house, just with a minor change in my emotion accompanied by a different mindset. Our dream home looked more like a nightmare. But I was up for the challenge and ready to take it on.

> *I had the ability to look at the old and visualise the new.*

It was D-day and we had succeeded. Failure was never really a consideration. Our conveyancer had now made the hefty transaction of $830,000. The prize: our wonderful new/old home. I received the call that the settlement had gone through and went to the agent to collect the keys. I don't know why, but for some reason I took the rental property manager from our agency with me, I think for some moral and emotional support. We pulled up outside and the former owners were still in the home still trying to remove their rubbish. They obviously didn't have the same luxury as us (funny how I can call it a luxury now) and had to do a simultaneous settlement, that is move out and move in, all on the same day.

We couldn't move in anyway because of the disgusting state of the property. Normally I would have said, "Take your time," but given the way that they had treated us that day as we pleaded for mercy, I couldn't bring myself to be my usual, nice self. Janet, a very young and confident property manager said, "Leave it with me." She went to the front door. "You have 15 minutes to get everything out of the house and onto the footpath," she stated. "Settlement has gone through and you are no longer the owners. Kindly remove everything or we will call the police—you are now trespassing." I have to say it felt good; even as I write it now it makes me chuckle a little. I am far from a vengeful person, but they had shown us no mercy. Not even so much as a kind word or a moment of compassion—now they were in *our* house. We didn't enforce our right to remove any of their things, but just having said it was sufficient and provided us with a little gratification. Who knows, maybe Janet didn't even say anything to them, but just believing she did was satisfying enough. People are always telling me karma is good, and that mine is coming. I always say, "I'm still waiting."

Over the next couple of weeks, we scrubbed our fingers to the bone. We even tried washing the walls, then painting them in the hope that the house would feel cleaner and fresher so that we could possibly rent it out, at least until our existing home was finally sold. You know what they say: "When the chips are down." Well, they really were. Having settled the new property, we were now drowning in debt. We had our existing mortgage (because of the lost investment we were unable to repay the debt) plus the new loan. I felt as though there was a row of dominos; someone had pushed the first one down and I was desperately trying to outrun them as they were crashing down around me. There just didn't seem to be any way to stop the chain reaction.

It was now March. With no offers, it was time to consider changing agents and time to re-auction our existing home of nine years. We didn't tell the auctioneer of our struggles, nor our desperation for money. We thought that if he had known our plight, he might try and convince us to sell for less or, worse still, tell everyone it was going to be a bargain. As a matter of fact, we never told our lender either, choosing instead to keep our struggles silent versus alerting them by asking for financial hardship. At this point in time, our trust in humanity was at its lowest point and we did everything in our power to try and protect what little we had left. The thought that they could force us to sell or try and repossess, despite our perfect mortgage conduct, kept us on our toes.

> *There just didn't seem to be any way to stop the chain reaction.*

It had only been a few months, yet we remained optimistic that our luck had to change for the better. I was somehow able to shuffle what little money we had each month and managed to keep up with all the mortgage repayments without ever defaulting. With the exception of those five family members who stood by our side, nobody was aware of our continued battle to remain afloat. This also made us think that, despite our begging for help only a few months earlier, nobody else thought to ever ask us if we could feed ourselves or our children. We can accept that they didn't want to risk their finances, but at a time when we were in what I would consider the biggest crisis of our lives, there were no offers of emotional support either. Had we been physically dying, as opposed to emotionally, would that have made a difference? Was it out of sheer guilt that they had abandoned us in our darkest moments, or was it because they secretly enjoyed seeing us lose everything? We personally feel it was the latter. We couldn't help but feel disappointed, hurt and angry—we would never have treated them that way. I have and will continue to want for others exactly what I would wish for myself; nothing more, nothing less. I guess that just makes us different people and we need to respect that others are simply not the same.

The auction ended with no bids. I left and went to our bedroom. I could no longer hide my pain. I was sobbing uncontrollably when suddenly the door flung open. It was the agent. He had seen me leave, and he wanted to reassure me that he would find a buyer. I couldn't hide it any longer. I turned to him with tears now streaming down my face. "You don't understand," I cried. "We are about one payment away from losing everything." I will never forget the shocked look on his face. He raced outside to see if he could convince the only interested buyer into making us an offer, but it was a no-go. We had so desperately wanted this time to be different. Surely, we couldn't continue to be plagued with bad luck. Something had to change, otherwise we would certainly be forced to sell the new home. Given the better location I saw this as our only other option, although at this point we didn't have any offers on either property. The new house posed a remote chance of possibly recouping some of our losses, even though it had been our plan for a new, more exciting future.

This was another major blow that again brought about the feelings of being cursed. In a suburb where everything sells, we had no interest and no offers to consider. If ever there was a time to lose my faith, it was now. How could it be that we were in a beachside suburb where even the dumpiest of houses were selling for astronomical prices, yet ours was so perfect, no cracks, solid as a rock and we had no buyers? It would have been so easy to feel that the world was against us. We were suffocating and there was nothing we could do to stop it.

We had no other option. Something had to give and so we were forced to list the new house for sale as well. At least now we would have a 50/50 chance of something selling and we would live in whichever house remained. We listed it for private sale for $850,000, a price that would allow us to recoup the cost of buying it, including stamp duty and agent fees for a sale. As luck would have it, the people across the road listed a "renovators delight". You know the kind—that beautiful,

They just killed any opportunity we had of selling our house.

old, double-fronted, Victorian property with old world charm and so much potential. Much to our disgust, instead of advertising it for its true value of $1 million-plus, they decided to go with $850,000-plus. Now the two "for sale" signs sat almost perfectly opposite each other in the street.

They just killed any opportunity we had of selling our house. That was exactly their plan; not to sabotage our sale as such, but to take advantage of potential buyers who would obviously make the comparison. It was clear that anyone looking to buy would compare the two and there was no comparison. Nobody would want to look at our mixed-fronted Californian bungalow when a property with a beautiful Victorian façade for the exact same price was available across the road. Finally, the auction day came for the other property and the street was lined with potential buyers all looking to grab a bargain. Admittedly it needed as much work as ours, but it had a different character; a wide entrance hall with two rooms either side, separated by double fireplaces and a gorgeous lace terraced veranda over-hanging the front porch. The bidding started, and it didn't take long to pass $950,000—already a far cry from ours. The property sold for $1,022,000. It would require a complete restoration, with a hefty bill attached to bring it back to its former glory. Weeks later, we finally received an offer on our existing home and we were able to move forward again.

You don't have any idea how much you have accumulated over the years until you need to move it all. With only months to go before our settlement we now faced the mammoth task of getting the house into a state in which we wanted to live in it ourselves. We now had a little money, as we had the deposit from the sale of our home and things were starting to sell. Things were far from rosy, nothing like the situation we had envisaged for ourselves just six months earlier. Instead of borrowing a little, we now had a much bigger debt than we would have liked, which meant that the renovations had to be done by us rather than contracting them out. I remember our friend Mario coming over every day and helping tear out the old horse-hair plaster, gutting the house to the frame. What a filthy job that was. Years of dust, grime and vermin were well-hidden in the ceiling cavity. Pulling it down, Mario looked like he had been doused in an explosion of dirty flour. Now, finally, we had a date to work towards and we needed to move quickly. With three small children, we needed to get everything in the new house renovated so that we could simply move in and not have dirt flying all over the place—at least that was the plan.

The house was not only dirty, but it was in its original state, bar one room, which had been tidied up a little. Do you remember those old 1950s kitchens with the timber cupboard doors that had the push button knobs? The floors were those beautiful old wide Baltic boards, but the gaps were big enough that the wind would blow through from under the house, along with the dirt, which you could see floating through the air when the sun shone. Remember the extension at the rear of the house where the dog had slept? It reeked of urine and was so disgusting it made me retch—it had to go. We pulled it right off, took the wrought iron from the roof and nailed it across the back of the house. This project would stretch us to our full capacity and we would do things we never thought we were capable of, like hanging plaster.

Neither my husband nor myself had done this before. We went to the local hardware store and hired a plaster lifter—not a person, but a contraption with a winder and many steel bars. There were some moments we laughed so hard as we argued, trying to decide whether it needed to be placed face up or down and then each trying to justify why we had that notion. If nothing else, it certainly brought us closer together as we spent every night hanging plaster. On the weekends, we would often put up flood lights so that we could continue plastering until two o'clock in the morning, just to get the house finished and habitable for us and the kids. We saved every penny we could and only paid for what we couldn't do ourselves, like the plumbing and electrics. The contract of sale stated that there was a permit for stumping which had only been done two years earlier, so we never thought to check that it had been done properly or that the stumps under the house were actually holding it up. When the floors were all ripped out, we could see that half of the stumps were either leaning sidewards, or not even making contact with the bearers. We ripped all the Baltic boards out of the house and sold them on eBay and laid hardwood floors because Baltic is soft, and we could see the kids, as good as they were, destroying it.

The next major learning curve for us was the ducted heating. The old house had relatively effective working ducted heating. However, during the house being dismantled this had been put out in the old garage at the back of the property. This garage was like something from an old movie; it was made up of wrought iron sheeting, adorned with golden rust patches. It certainly looked like it had seen better days. The previous owners had raked the leaves in the back yard. Hard to believe, as I don't think they had ever otherwise cleaned a day in their lives. Next to the garage was a pile of old grass clippings and leaves—it must've been four feet deep. The more we looked, the more rubbish we found. The back yard looked like a junk heap with

Thank God for Google, which enabled my husband and I to reconstruct the ducted system.

crap everywhere. You could hardly move. I wrenched open the old tin sliding door and there lay the ducted heating, in what seemed like a thousand pieces. I put my head in my hands and cried. I had planned to go out to the garage and drag the long hoses back under the house but now they lay separated from the connectors and I had no idea where to begin.

Thank God for Google, which enabled my husband and I to reconstruct the ducted system. That night I sat on a camping chair in the cold and drew a picture of each connector. Then I cut out each one and taped the pictures one-by-one, like a jigsaw puzzle back together. Then I numbered each piece accordingly. "No, you need to duct tape 3 and 4 together on the left side, not the right!" We did it; together, we had successfully reinstalled the ducted heating and better still it worked just fine. This alone saved us thousands of dollars, not having to pay someone to come and do it for us. At the same time, there was an auction company nearby in South Melbourne selling brand new kitchens with full stone bench tops. I went to a few auctions and finally managed to secure us a new kitchen for a very affordable price, around half that of a custom-made kitchen. I bargained and got all the appliances for rock-bottom prices, even scoring a brand new free-standing 900mm oven/stove for only $2300. The house was finally coming together; we now had a new bathroom, kitchen, dining room, lounge, two bedrooms and half a family room, which had the washing machine in it. It was spotlessly clean, but it certainly wasn't complete.

It was now the end of July 2006 and we were in the middle of winter, with the most challenging times nearly behind us. My baby girls were turning five and they were at my mother's house, over an hour's drive away. We couldn't afford to take the time out to drive up and back to see them as we were working our butts off trying desperately to finish the house before we had to move out of our existing home. As a mother, it still brings tears to my eyes as I recollect my mother's words as she spoke to me on the phone that day. "I haven't told the girls it's their birthday today," she said, calmly. "They won't know if you tell them next week. Maybe we should just wait until they come home, and you can celebrate then?" My heart broke in two. It was hard to hold it all together. It was our girls' birthday and I had to pretend it wasn't. I managed to compose myself enough to get on with the job at hand.

Finally, the project was coming together, and we could now see light at the end of the tunnel. It was August 2006 and moving day came around far too quickly. We moved into the house; it was cosy to say the least. All our possessions were now stacked in boxes up to the ceiling. Don't forget, the ceilings were 10 feet high—we had a lot of crap. That winter was extremely cold. We had moved into the house, but the back was boarded up with the steel sheets that we had taken from the horrible extension that we demolished, so there were gaps everywhere. The heating was working extra hard but it was escaping through the cracks. When we had the new hardwood floors laid, I had asked them to finish the floorboards by staggering the ends using alternating lengths, so that when it came time to add the extension on, it didn't have a straight line where the two would later meet. Feeling the wind blowing up through the gaps, I realised this had been a bad idea. We tried everything to close the holes and even tried using the off-cuts to slot into the gaps to try and overcome the wind. In the end, going to bed early and using electric blankets was the only way.

> *Finally, the project was coming together, and we could now see light at the end of the tunnel.*

On the other hand, the summer proved even more challenging. The wrought iron would heat up in summer sun, so staying cool proved an even more difficult challenge than finding warmth in the winter. Within a few short months, our investment properties were sold, the house had settled, and normality was starting to return to our lives. We signed a building contract and added a much-needed extension onto the back of the house. Life was not without its challenges, but we were all still together and things were progressing nicely. Upon completion of the extension our new home was now full of possibilities. We had succeeded and could put the worst behind us—or so it seemed.

6

The New Normal

*"Attitude is more important than the past, than education,
than money, than circumstances, than what people do or say.
It is more important than appearance, giftedness, or skill."*

— CHARLES R. SWINDOLL

Every day for the past eight months had been hard, mentally and physically. The toll it was taking on my body was also becoming more evident and my symptoms were now a learned behaviour for my body. Any time I was exposed to an uncomfortable situation, my body now threw itself into a panic attack. I fought hard to try and control them. I was so determined, but it wasn't going to be easy. They say time heals all, but as each day passed it began to feel more and more like we were cursed. It was difficult to wake up each day feeling like we were being punished. I pushed myself to the limit and through the pain more often than I could bear. Tears were still a daily ritual and so too were the panic attacks. Never in my life, prior to that December day had I ever experienced a panic attack, and now they were coming at an alarming rate.

Simply going to the letterbox brought on an attack. I think it was the fear it would contain bills. The simple task of logging into our bank account and seeing our debts was also enough to trigger an attack, not to mention the agony of wondering how I was going to balance the books each week. Paying the bills and the mortgage caused me extreme stress, and attack after attack. Nobody, with the exception of a few close people, really knew of our pain. We had hidden it all; we were embarrassed. Frank particularly struggled with his pride. He couldn't cope with anyone knowing, and so I too had to keep it a secret. He took all the personal criticisms to heart. On the contrary, I continued to remind him that if we'd known things weren't right, we wouldn't have done it. He didn't say much, but deep down I know he suffered emotionally too. Each of us has our own coping mechanism and what works for one doesn't necessarily work for the other. In a partnership, it's important to understand that each of us handles the same situation differently. Until recently, we had continued to keep it hidden from the outside world, sucking the pain up and swallowing it.

After a few months, we still had very little money and were now trying to pay two mortgages instead of one.

After a few months, we still had very little money and were now trying to pay two mortgages instead of one. I was now working part-time in a call centre for the credit card collections department at one of the major banks, seeing mortgage customers at night and working in a factory an hour away in Melton one night a week. My cousin Julie had found this job for herself and with a little convincing she managed to get me in too. My personality really struggles with repetitive, non-thinking work; it drives me crazy and yet here I was, hanging gutter clips on a moving conveyor. To keep my mind active and stimulated I tried all sorts of mental games. I struggled with the monotony, but I had a new money plan and this formed a part of it. I love fast-paced, mind-challenging work with a twist of innovation or creativity, so this was not ideal. I was extremely grateful, because it did pay money and I needed every cent of it to help pay the bills. I forced myself to be inspired. Actually, something good did come of it; a little hidden gem which I almost forgot to tell you. I scored a kitchen sink. I can't remember what was wrong with it but it was insignificant and certainly not noticeable. That certainly made up for all the repetitive work.

We were extremely lucky because Frank was able to continue his daily routine, going to work every day as if nothing had happened. I don't know what I would have done had he not been able to cope or go to work every day; he was really a silent soldier—our saviour. I doubt he even mentioned it to any of his work colleagues. He's quiet and likes to keep things on the inside. On the other hand, I'm a talker. It's my only refuge. I need to get it out, talk things through. I often found myself feeling like that bottle of champagne that had been shook up. The cork was about to pop and I was desperately trying to keep the screws tight. Working from home alone most of the time, I had no one to talk to and it was putting extra pressure on me. I was a mother; I was expected to be the nurturer, yet I so desperately needed someone to nurture me. Someone who supported me, despite what now appeared to be poor decisions. Decisions that, ultimately, I had contributed to. I started to be consumed by guilt again. Was this all my fault? Even though we have always made every decision together I somehow felt guilty for wanting our children's lives to be better than our own.

I knew I had to do something. I was snapping at the kids and something had to change. My poor babies were so good, but something as simple as asking me, "Mummy, we're hungry, what can we eat?" pushed me over the edge. I felt like I was being pulled from side to side, like an elastic band that had run out of stretch and was about to snap in two. It was time for me to acknowledge that I couldn't do it alone. I am an extremely strong woman, but I had to reach out for help. Finally I gave in, called the local doctors surgery and asked to see a female doctor. She was new, in her 60's and very kind. She took the time to listen to my story. Amazingly enough, at that exact point in time her very own daughter had just been diagnosed with fibromyalgia. "It sounds like you have what my daughter has," she said, and sent me home to read up on the condition via the Mayo Clinic in the USA. Finally, at 40 years of age, someone had hit the jackpot.

As I read up on the symptoms of the disease, I now had a real explanation for my life-long sickness, rating myself an 8.5 out of 10 for the symptoms suffered by most fibromyalgia patients. Then the hurt set in; knowing I had spent the past four decades going undiagnosed and made to feel like it was all in my head. In the past, doctors had told me that I should seek psychiatric help, but instead I changed doctors. I knew deep in my heart that all my symptoms were real, but those doctors had certainly caused me to question myself over the years. I now had a true sense of relief and it changed me moving forward. That day she also recommended I start taking Effexor, an antidepressant. Initially I hesitated and asked if there were any side effects. She told me that she herself was on them and that they would help calm me. She handed me two sample packs to get me started. I didn't like the thought of taking them. I noticed that my reactions seemed to be a little slower, giving me more time to process things. Unfortunately, it didn't stop the panic attacks. I

I hated that my body produced tears as a coping mechanism and had hoped that the medication would stop that.

hated that my body produced tears as a coping mechanism and had hoped that the medication would stop that. One thing I still find frustrating is that, particularly when someone is suffering financial hardship, they have to endure the added expense of going to the doctor and sometimes buying much-needed medication, which is so expensive.

My doctor prescribed an anti-depressant for me at $75 per month, yet I was struggling financially and only needed it because it would help keep me sane. The very reason I was at the doctors in the first place was because of the panic attacks which were the result of us not having enough money, yet the drugs I needed were going to cost me even more—money we didn't have. At one point I begged Centrelink to consider whether they could assess our case. I desperately needed a health care card to keep the cost of medication and doctor visits down, but because my husband was still working we failed to qualify as he earned a few dollars over the cut-off point.

A couple of months passed and summer was here. I tried on my one-piece bathers. *What happened?* They didn't fit anymore. How could I have gained so much weight so quickly? Worse still, how was it that I didn't even notice the weight gain, especially as I was particularly weight-conscious? I had started the medication only a few months earlier, weighing only 67 kilograms and now I was 80 kilograms. As if I wasn't already depressed enough. I realised that the anti-depressant pills had slowed my metabolism, almost to a halt, and this had caused me to stack on all this weight in a very short space of time. To add to my frustration was the fact that I had even asked the doctor if there were any side effects, particularly around weight gain and she had assured me that there were not. I was once again fighting to lose all that extra weight. Instantly upon making the connection that the drugs were the cause of my weight gain, I began halving the dose without consulting the doctor first. I didn't need anyone telling me not to do it. I experienced a few flying black spots, but it was worth it. I needed to get back into shape. If only it was that easy.

It didn't work. Losing weight proved to be more difficult than raising the money for the settlement. Now I was left feeling disgusted at myself for all the extra weight I was carrying. I realised that I was looking to food as a coping mechanism. One thing led to another and now I was addicted to chocolate. I think you will see that I am perfectly qualified to talk about every aspect of money and the link it has with your health, relationships and general wellbeing. I

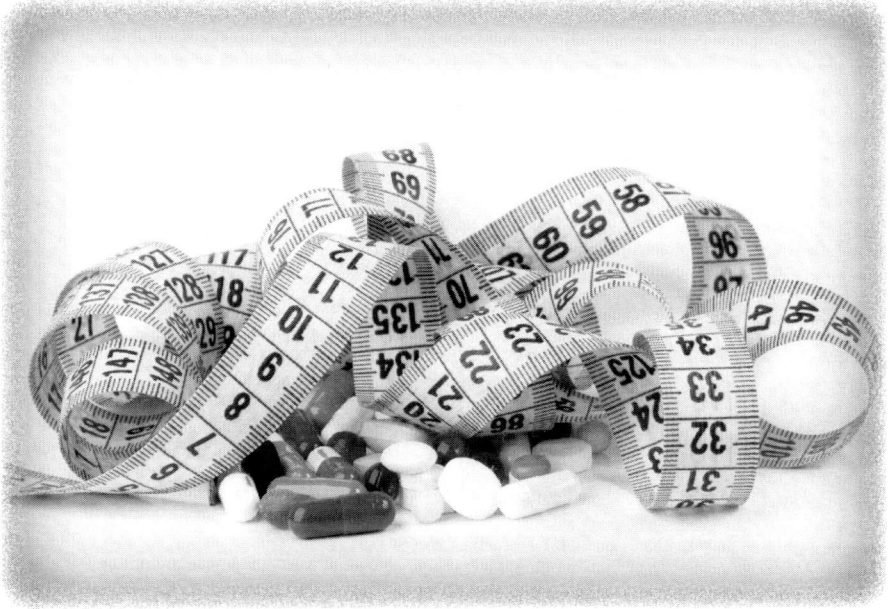

had now experienced an array of emotions and physical traps, of the mind, body and spirit. Thinking back, I still wondered how we managed to do it.

Fast forward another couple of years to the end of September 2008. Despite never missing a repayment, never receiving a default and thankfully avoiding the need to declare bankruptcy, we were still a little fragile, with a mortgage larger than we could ever have expected. We were on top of it all, but outside our home, the money world was like a ticking time bomb. I was seeing mortgage clients again, having left the real estate job after only a few short months to concentrate on the renovations. Clients were beginning to panic, telling me that they wanted to fix their home loan interest rates for fear that rates would once again return to figures previously seen in the late 1980's. Of course, it didn't matter what I thought, they were all reflecting on what had been, so I could only explain to them what I was seeing. I was of the belief that things were very different to those times. I believed the greater population, or marketplace as I refer to it, could not continue to sustain the current interest rates, which back then were climbing towards 9.45% p.a. It was my theory that general living expenses were so much higher compared with those in the late 80's and that this, combined with mounting petrol costs and household utility bills, meant that the economy was hugely different. I explained that, when accompanied by increasing mortgage interest rates, in my opinion the market was headed for a huge crash and it wasn't just on the horizon, but in the immediate future. One after the other, I tried desperately to stop customers from fixing their home loans, many of whom thankfully listened to me.

However, one lovely young couple insisted that they wanted to fix their home loan at 9.15% for five years, just a week before the Global Financial Crisis hit. I tried desperately to sway them, insisting that if they absolutely must fix, to consider a three-year term instead. They went with five years. I cringed and watched on as they told me that their parents had seen it all before. A week later, the market crashed and the call that I had been dreading came—it was them. "I know you said not to fix," they said, politely. "But is there anything we can do?" They acknowledged that I had advised against it, but that didn't help their situation. The only saving grace was that this loan had the added benefit of allowing a 100% offset with the fixed rate. The fee to exit was some $23,000 despite only having a small loan of $198,000. Unfortunately, they had little choice but to ride it out to avoid being hit.

Looking back now, I believe the hardest part of our personal financial distress was the calls I had to make requesting hardship. Never in our lives had we needed to ask for anything. Money was always plentiful and yet at the most difficult and emotional time in our lives when our world was collapsing around us, I needed to make those dreadful calls. When the council rates arrived, on the back of the notice there was a number to call for hardship, so I finally plucked up the courage and called the number. "How dare you ask for hardship when you have two properties in Williamstown?" the voice at the other end spat at me. As if it wasn't hard enough for me to pick up that phone, I now had to deal with this horrible woman who had prejudged me. I tried to explain what we had been caught up in when she interrupted me. "You need to make an appointment to see a financial counsellor." Thankfully, he was much more compassionate and showed empathy towards our situation. He asked me what the problem was. "I know how to manage money," I stated. "The problem I have right now is I just don't have enough of it to pay everything. That will change once our house sells." His concern was evident; he signed off on the agreement, allowing us to make instalments until our property sale was finalised. What frustrated me—and in turn engaged my passion—was that he also explained that, as my husband was working full-time, he could not provide us with further financial

Looking back now, I believe the hardest part of our personal financial distress was the calls I had to make requesting hardship.

counselling as we did not qualify because financial counselling is only available where neither party is employed.

Next call, the girls' kindergarten. Again, prejudice. Nobody understood, nobody cared. No-one really wanted to know—oh, but they did. "Why are your girls not attending kinder?" they would pry. I tried, in vain, to explain that I had no choice but to send them to their grandmother, who lived more than an hour away, as we could not care for them at the time. It fell on deaf ears. They only heard what they wanted to hear. They had no compassion that our house was in tatters. Our money situation? Forget it. Our son was different; he was of school age and it was compulsory for him to attend school during the day. I called the Catholic primary school that he attended and they happily wrote off the final term's fee, which was a huge relief. Finally some compassion from the church—it was very humbling. There was only a couple of hundred dollars left outstanding as I had already struggled desperately to pay the majority before plucking up the courage to ask for help. Nonetheless, I was extremely grateful. Now the electricity bill could be paid.

I continued to do my best and paid everyone every single penny that was owed. The occasional care was different to the others; they knew me well and that I was good for every cent, so they allowed me to pay them after the dust had settled. I paid them the following year and the kindness they showed me was invaluable. In difficult financial times there are supposedly measures in place to provide assistance, but accessing it is often the hardest part. On another occasion, I forced myself to walk into a local Centrelink office. I stood strong in front of the wall of assistance brochures, when I was approached by a female employee, who politely asked me if I needed help. I tried to ask her what we would be entitled to when she said, "You work out what you think you are entitled to, tell me and I will let you know." Then she glared at me and, with an angry tone, said, "Why don't you try getting a job, like me?" I could hardly believe my ears. I had to leave and quickly, as I was about to burst into tears yet again. I lowered my sunglasses that were nestled in my hair to cover my eyes and made a dash for the door.

Empowering yourself to reach out for help can be overwhelming, even at the best of times. My objective for writing this is to show you that giving up is the easy solution. I could have said *it's all too hard, I can't do it*, sit in the corner and cry. I cried, there's no denying that, but I think losing a million dollars is enough to make anyone cry. What I want you to focus on is your *mindset*. I had pushed myself, refusing to give up and I had continued to set a new money plan for us. I looked at the end point and worked backwards, asking myself: *how much do we need? When do we need it by?* By breaking it down into smaller chunks we could set about the task of raising the money. After settling the house it would have been much simpler to sell and walk away, count our losses

> *Empowering yourself to reach out for help can be overwhelming, even at the best of times.*

and start over. Assessing our position, there were so many options, including staying in the home that we already loved so much. There was a point when it looked like we could sell the newly-acquired house rather than our existing home. Without our money plan we would not have been able to piece together our future, which may have led to us missing our greatest opportunity to salvage more money. By having a plan in place, we were able to visualise a future and see that, with a long-term plan, putting in the hard yards at the new place, we would hopefully restore our finances over a period of time.

I have never been one to give up, no matter how hard the day ahead looks. By focusing on what you really want and planning to see it through, or better still to excel, I believe you will never fail. I guess the other important aspects of success are to focus on looking for things you love, be with people that inspire you and avoid those that bring you down. It's always far harder to build a strong, positive attitude and mindset when you are surrounded by people who aspire to be or do nothing. Of course, that doesn't mean you need to hang out with rock stars or rich people—although that does sound fun—just fair, honest, inspiring and motivated people. Never compromise your values; just keep on track and never lose sight of the dream. Remember, there is a real difference between a dream and a goal. A dream is not necessarily realistic or achievable, whereas a goal should be measurable and within reach.

7

Moving Forward

"The only way to get love is to be lovable. It's very irritating if you have a lot of money. You'd like to think you could write a check: 'I'll buy a million dollars' worth of love.' But it doesn't work that way. The more you give love away, the more you get."

— WARREN BUFFETT

Letting go of the past is the hardest thing to do. We'd come through the most difficult of times, and now we could see the light at the end of the tunnel. However, it was time to reassess our future yet again. We loved our neighbours, we loved the location, but it was just a house. I did the maths and although we could cope, there just seemed to be too many what-ifs; too many factors that lay outside of our control like the constant hype of interest rate increases and falling property prices. No longer did we want to risk putting our lives at the mercy of others, instead choosing to be in control of our own destiny.

It was 2010 and selling seemed like the obvious choice. We would buy a slightly cheaper home, reduce our debt and enjoy life with the kids while they were still young. We listed the house and, although it did take longer than we would have liked, it eventually sold. We were debt free and things were looking up. We spent countless hours roaming the suburbs to find that perfect new home, but it proved a lot harder than we expected. We wanted to remain in Williamstown, only downgrade a little. Again, nothing ticked all the boxes on our must-have list. We drove everywhere in an attempt to find the right house for us and ended up in the next suburb over. One night, we drove past a "for sale" sign; the house seemed a little overrun but it looked like a good-sized plot of land. This seventies-style house would be our next home. With a bit of a clean-up it was good enough to move into as is, but I knew that it would be too difficult to modify once we were living in the house, so we undertook the mammoth task of another full renovation in just 64 days. We gutted the entire house, removing everything, including the exterior windows, changing them all to modern timber windows. We reframed the inside of the house, installed new plasterboard, electrics, plumbing, kitchen and bathrooms—the works. I literally became a builder's labourer again, learning how to jackhammer the marble tiles off concrete slab and even stretching myself to screw the decking on so that we could fill our newly-built pool with water before our first Christmas in the new house.

At that point we could easily have paid cash for a nice, new two-storey house with all the bells and whistles in a cheaper outer suburb like Point Cook, Tarneit or Truganina for around $750,000, but I knew we needed an updated money plan if we were ever going to retire with money in the bank. If we paid cash, we wouldn't need a mortgage and we could start saving again immediately, but how much could we realistically save during that time, while still enjoying life and travelling the world? We needed to trust our gut feeling and take a gamble. It seemed like the only logical option was to invest in a large piece of land in a better location, that would be more likely to appreciate in value, giving us more choices when we reached retirement, which was moving ever closer.

Moving day came around once again and despite making the decision to leave, it was a very sad day. We had never imagined ever leaving Williamstown and now we were loading up trucks and moving to another suburb. For some this may seem insignificant, but for us it was almost as though our dreams were once again being somewhat destroyed. We had spent the first four years of our marriage dreaming about moving to Williamstown and now, after almost 13 years, we had to leave. It was the end of an era. We were only moving seven kilometres away, but we were still leaving the suburb behind, and with increasing prices, we believed the chances of returning were slim.

Moving day came around once again and despite making the decision to leave, it was a very sad day.

Moving into the next suburb also came with a slight mind-shift. Suddenly, we were faced with questions like, "Why would you move from Williamstown to *there*?" When we first got married, we lived in Hoppers Crossing. People would ask, "So where do you live?" Hearing the answer, they would suddenly lose interest in the conversation. Were people really judging me based on where I lived? It happened more than once so it wasn't my imagination. Perception is reality. Somehow, it seemed that where I lived played an important role in their assessment of me. I still struggle with that concept.

We purchased our first property in South Williamstown back in 1994, just two years after we got married—a tiny, little dump of a house, I might add. It was barely standing. I decided to do an experiment. The next time someone asked me where I lived, I would say, "We just bought an old house in Williamstown that we are going to tear down and rebuild new." "Wow, really?!" was the typical response I received from most and they were intrigued to hear more about it. Suddenly, people were interested in pursuing a

longer conversation with me. For the next 13 years, Williamstown would remain our home; time after time, being asked where I lived, I could respond with the answer they wanted to hear.

Now, we were on the move again, and I began seeing similar reactions as people asked me, "Why would you leave Willy?" as they affectionately referred to it. At the time, I laughed it off, preferring to keep our secret. "We want to travel the world," I would say. "The house we bought enables us to do all of that and it's still close to the beach, so we have the best of both worlds." As enthusiastic as I sounded, I still needed to convince myself. Unfortunately, my son still went to school in Williamstown, so the recovery period seemed like it would go on forever. Stupid, I know, but let me be clear: we didn't want to move back because of what people would say—we just really loved living there. I suppose you would have to see it to understand. Williamstown is quaint whereas where we live now is being overrun with new townhouse developments. On the flip side it has turned out to be a good land investment.

A year or so after we made the move, and having transferred the girls to the school at the end of the street, I decided it was time to sell their old school uniforms. I placed an advertisement and shortly after I received a call from a lovely English lady who had just relocated to Australia. "What a lovely street this is," she commented, standing on my doorstep. "You can see the beach at the end, much like the street we are moving into." "I know," I responded. "We just moved from a street much like this in Williamstown." We looked at each other and wondered if we were talking about the same street. In unison, we both said the street name. Unbelievable—she was moving into our old street. *How coincidental*, we thought. It gets better. "You aren't moving into number 21 are you?" I asked. "Yes!" she said. "Were you the ones that renovated the house?" I nodded and smiled. She told me how excited she was to be moving into my old house. Instantly I could feel the emotions building up and I think she could sense it too. I told her what had happened to us and that we had never wanted, nor planned to leave. She insisted that I pay her a visit. "Thank you," I replied. "I appreciate it but to be honest, I'm not sure I could handle it." Living there was our dream and leaving it behind had been so hard. With that, we parted ways.

> *Living there was our dream and leaving it behind had been so hard.*

It was time to start putting the past behind us and create a new plan. No longer would we dwell on what might have been and instead focus on the real reason why we chose to move. From this, our new money plan was created. We would allow ourselves a budget of around $100,000 towards travelling around the world with the kids. For the first time since 2005, our life was finally taking shape again and we could start enjoying holidays as we had once before.

CHAPTER

8

Who Are You Without Your Story?

You don't know what you don't know??

Just when I thought I'd seen it all, a huge development in the study of my passion was around the corner. Here's a little mind-twister for you. It's funny how we often take for granted the things we know. Let's explore this for a moment.

> You know what you know.
> You know what you don't know. But...
> *you don't know what you don't know.*

What does that even mean, you might ask yourself? The third aspect is quite revealing. Until you discover new information you didn't know, usually you are oblivious to the fact that it was missing from your knowledge bank. Have you ever discovered new information, totally amazed that you'd never learned it before? Fast forward 10 years, and I knew I desperately wanted to formally launch my courses to the general public, so that I could reach out to more people. Managing money is paramount to our wellbeing and far too many people are suffering unnecessarily due to a lack of money management skills. Furthermore, I knew I had the knowledge, skills and personal experience necessary, but what I didn't realise at the time was that a breakthrough was on the horizon. I was about to discover what I call the intrinsic missing link in the equation that I desperately sought to add to my courses.

That vital link for me, was realising that the missing piece for most customers is the ability to untangle negative life events— or stories, as I prefer to call them. Being able to change direction isn't easy. If you can dissect your stories, you can find and identify common feelings or attachments and discover patterns in your own behaviour, which can then be addressed, conquered and repurposed into positive outcomes. Most of us understand that maintaining a sunny outlook and creating healthy thoughts leads to better outcomes, but achieving this can be much harder than it appears. However, I believe that by carefully combining your core values with your mindset, together with your money matters, you can have them form a new strong bond that blends nicely. You should also start to see improvements in how you manage your relationships at home and at work.

I knew that this had enhanced my ability, not only to recover, but to cope through the bad times. I now also grasped the concept that, by continuing to constantly create and maintain new, manageable and achievable money plans, I was always evolving and heading towards a new goal. This has proven invaluable in ensuring that I remained driven and focused on new and exciting experiences. I had created a bucket list without being aware of it and, better still, I was ticking off the list one by one. These goals have acted as a constant distraction and helped get me through when the bills were piling up. I am constantly trying to better empower people to deal with everyday problems. I often explore new mindset strategies and develop concepts to expand my clients' views towards greater achievements; those goals that ultimately help them to grow. I would like to share with you how I discovered this vital missing link.

It was mid-November 2014. I had just attended a conference in the city and leaving late that night, I chatted with a few attendees on my way back to my car. It was a cool night and, as we walked briskly to our cars just to keep warm, we stopped briefly and huddled together. At that moment, a gentleman from the group, who I had stood next to during the entire conference that weekend, gently leaned in towards me and, in a quiet but firm voice, said, "Belinda, who are you without your story?" I moved my head from side to side. You know, like you do when you are pondering the question being asked of you. It felt as though he had reached in deep and grabbed

It felt as though he had reached in deep and grabbed at my very soul, giving it a little shake, but in a kind and positive way.

at my very soul, giving it a little shake, but in a kind and positive way. He had given me a wake-up call that I didn't even realise I hadn't yet answered. My foundations were shifted forever.

I have always been the type of person to question everything and this was one of those *a-ha* moments, where the learning curve would be so big it would almost instantly change who I was moving forward. I had spent my forty-something years learning from everything, and there have been a few too many trials and tribulations, but this would prove to be one of the most enlightening questions I'd ever been asked. "What do you mean?" I asked quietly, as the tears welled up in my eyes and my voice began to quiver. He again prompted me, only this time with a little more assertion. "Who are you without your story?" I again told him, only this time I was a little angrier, not with him but with myself. I thought I had worked hard on myself already, that I had it mostly covered. "I really don't understand what you mean." He replied, "I think you do." Starting to cry, I jumped into my car. Before I could even start the engine and begin the long drive home, I sat quietly and reflected on the question.

> *Looking into the night sky, deep inside me I felt sick as I contemplated what the answers to that question might be.*

Looking into the night sky, deep inside me I felt sick as I contemplated what the answers to that question might be. He had prompted me to ask myself over and over again in my mind, "Who am I?" What relevance or impact does my story have on who I am? My head throbbed; it felt

as though it would explode as my mind span at a million miles per hour. I had to get home, so I needed to pull myself together to make the journey home safely. It was now almost midnight and it had been a long and exhausting conference. I sighed, took a few deep breaths and turned the radio up high, just high enough so that the vibrations didn't make my ears ring. I love music and it sustained me enough to drive home.

I hardly slept that night as I tossed and turned, churning over the past events of my life with the words ringing in my head over and over. My story. "Who am I without my story?" I would spend the next few days indulging in my story. My father left when I was only six years old and I had never fully accepted how he could just turn his back and walk away. This thought again bewildered me especially after having my own children. My grandfather, who was like a real father to me, died at the age of 67. My first boss after I left school at 16 was constantly verbally abusive towards me. He would call me an idiot for missing out a word of my shorthand—it was all very demeaning. Then we lost all our money. The stories just kept flowing one after the other, each taking me back to a point in my life that was traumatic and ultimately bringing me to tears. As I relived each and every one of those painful memories, it didn't take long to see the pattern emerging. All these stories had consumed me, whether consciously or not, and each one carried a pain, a weight, often too heavy to carry.

> *I always believed that my knowledge of numbers was a gift. A born talent.*

Emotionally, I was challenged by all these events. I had survived each of them and with each one came a learning curve, but each one also chipped a little bit of me away. When I was younger, I thought I understood the impact that my story had on me, particularly that of my father leaving. This forced me to readdress my true feelings. I had never really made the connection as to the deeper effects and, ultimately, the solution needed to overcome my fears.

It was only after I began helping to empower others to take control of their money that I started to see behavioural patterns emerging, which challenged me well into my forties to work harder on myself so that I could be more powerful in assisting others. I started exploring deeper into my own history and by asking myself, "Who am I without my story?" I began to realise that within my behaviours there may be an underlying, unresolved issue that kept arising. It seemed that I had survived using my only coping mechanism—my voice. If I could talk it out, it was out, and each story was substituted by the next as my life continued to unfold. On the outside, I covered up the pain. People would often ask me, "What drugs are you on?" I was confused by that comment and couldn't understand what they meant. "You're always happy!" they'd say. Despite everything that was taken from me I have always insisted that the one thing I can't be robbed of is my smile. I own that—it's mine. It's been the one thing that keeps me strong. So, when I was asked that mind-boggling question late that night, it would prove to be the biggest but most rewarding question I'd ever heard. It held the answers to the many unanswered questions I still had, answers that I desperately sought. Ultimately, it would also be my gift to you.

I took a journey back into my past and what surprised me most is that finally I started lining up all the ducks, so to speak. I began to see things more deeply rather than as they appeared on the surface. As I mentioned earlier, I have always been inclined to question and over-analyse things way too much. I never could accept that "shit happens", instead preferring to believe that everything in life happens for a reason. My faith is strong. I believe in God—in *my* God. I believe that he has guided me to where I am today. However, if I am to continue to believe this and grow in my faith, then I also must believe that things really do happen for a reason to teach us important lessons. I can also help others change their lives with this very knowledge that I have suffered to gain. Our faith is most challenged when times are hard. "If there really is a God why would he make people suffer?" It's so easy to fall into this trap. Blame never produces a fabulous outcome. The greatest learning curves come through challenging times, but only if you embrace change.

We should be grateful when life finds us well but it's the difficult times that force us to stray and question our faith the most.

I always believed that my knowledge of numbers was a gift. A born talent. However the more I explored, the more I realised that there was no such thing as a born talent. I had spent a lifetime training myself without consciously being aware of my constant thirst for learning. Suddenly, I began to understand that my knowledge, that I once took for granted, that I had given away so freely, was in fact an unpaid, unnamed qualification, rather than a talent bestowed upon me by God. Whilst others were attending universities, obtaining or enriching their knowledge from other peoples' thoughts via books and the like, I was out there, living real experiences first-hand and taking the hard knocks that would ultimately grant me the expertise to truly make a difference in the lives of so many as they crossed my path over the years. Some may disagree—that's ok. I can accept that, but often psychology gained from books doesn't always teach perspective. Sure, it may point out cause and effect, but it doesn't necessarily evoke a sense of understanding and compassion. Mental pain, suffering and anguish resulting from life experiences reveal themselves in obscure ways. Truly understanding why people behave in certain ways is complex. However, I have found that teaching them how to comprehend their own behaviours and identify underlying events can help them understand themselves.

By learning to deal with confronting feelings and emotions, and their often-adverse impact, they can implement strategies to avoid recurring habits, especially where money comes into play. I was fully educated by first-hand work experience and each of the traumas in my life have provided me with not just insight, but compassion, empathy and understanding, allowing me to offer solutions that I knew would work, without pretending to understand someone else's pain or lecture people on how to fix their lives with useless solutions.

In my desperate quest to seek out and conquer my own demons, I first needed to understand what they were. This may seem easy, but it was one of those big ugly life questions. I started to unravel the commonalities and symptoms that drew me to underlying behaviours that ultimately triggered emotions that I hated. They had learned to camouflage themselves so well that even I had missed the clues. I wanted to know why I would burst into tears in a confronting situation. So where did this come from? I needed to pinpoint the source. I knew that my father leaving had left a real bruise. Was this the cause? All I needed to do was connect the dots. What I discovered was amazing. Whenever I felt threatened, the fear of failure or rejection was the effect. So how and why did they connect? Let's take the horrible boss as an example.

I now realise I am good at languages and everyday math, and shorthand was just another language really.

I'm a 16-year-old girl sitting at an old timber desk in a flashy law firm, thrown in at the deep end. Thrown into the big wide world, fresh out of high school. My new workspace was a rough old wooden desk, with four thin legs to support it and a small drawer underneath where I could put some stationery. On it sat an old, green IMB electric typewriter. I didn't think I was all that good at typing, which probably didn't help. I never really wanted to be a secretary either. I hadn't chosen typing as a subject in year 10, so to get up to speed, or so my mother thought, she enrolled me at night school one night per week whilst I attended school full-time during the day.

It was a real chore dragging myself to that class each week. Everyone in the class was super-fast and I was not. If I close my eyes, I can still picture myself sitting in that room. There must have been at least 30 old manual typewriters on desks only just big enough to hold them. Six rows of five and the teacher standing up front. The teacher would say "Go!" and all I could hear was the clattering of the keys and the loud clunk as each student quickly flicked the return handle. The noise was loud and somewhat daunting as I was plodding along so slowly. It wasn't the noise but more so the fact that I knew this meant that they were quickly moving down the page, while I would still be on only the first line. We were supposed to be able to copy type from the book on our left, but I would constantly lose my place because instead of typing whilst looking at the book, I would read the words, then look at the keys and type what I had read, then desperately try and find my place on the page again. I never wanted to be a secretary, but I loved shorthand and I was good at it. I was top of my class at school in Year 10, and let's face it—who doesn't like being good at something? By the time I left school I could do 120 words per minute. I now realise I am good at languages and everyday math, and shorthand was just another language really.

A few little hidden treasures about me. Going back to the office, I was tucked away in a quiet little office with Pam. I think the room was only about two, maybe two-and-a-half metres wide and only the same in depth. Rather claustrophobic. God forbid if the door had shut. My desk was to the right of the door and I sat with my back to Pam, whose desk was behind mine. Pam was a shorter woman, in her 40s. She was sweet, very softly spoken and well-mannered. Some 34 years later I couldn't tell you what her job title was. She wasn't HR, but she was given the task of supervising the new kid. One morning she came in and said to me, "Belinda, Peter wants you in his office to take shorthand." Gathering my pen and notebook, I quickly walked to his office, which was only a few metres across the hall. I sat on one of the chairs opposite his desk. He was a partner in the law firm I was now employed by and he was a very well-known family lawyer. His office had a window and he thought he was a cut above the rest. He was straight to the point and didn't have time to make small talk. I was his slave; I was there to perform a job and get out. He spoke at such a quick speed for the dictation. Maybe he felt he had to speak that fast simply to get all the information out of his head as quickly as possible. He dictated, or should I say rambled on, and hardly took a breath as he dictated six letters, one after the other. I went back to my office almost relieved that it had stopped. It was only my first week on the job and, although I had learned shorthand at school, this was my first time in a real-life setting and with the legal language it was all very new to me. I typed up the letters at my desk, desperately trying to remember what this one word was. Pam came into the office and I told her I was having trouble with one word. She suggested that I go back and ask Peter, which I did.

Peter said to me, "Did you tell Ron Knightsbridge you could take shorthand or not?" "Yes," I responded quietly. "I did," to which he abruptly shouted at me, "You are a liar! You can't even read your own handwriting." I fought hard to hold back the tears. I wasn't a liar! I had missed one word. He was the boss from hell. With my tail between my legs, like a scared and frightened dog, I found my way back to my desk and struggled to hold it all together. Pam returned, and the tension must have been so thick you could cut the air with a knife. She sat behind me and, even with my back to her, she could see straight through me. "Is everything okay?" she enquired. In a broken and quivering voice I told her what had happened. She was very upset. She immediately stormed out of the room and over to Peter's office. I couldn't hear what she said but she returned shortly after and said, "Peter said to apologise to you and when he sees you he will tell you himself." Peter never did see me after that day. He made sure to look at the ground every time our paths crossed. The foundations for intimidation were laid that day and would continue for many years to come.

Prompted by the looming question, "Who am I without my story?" I realised that this event with Peter had a common thread to that of my father leaving. Threatened and scared, I had retreated to a feeling of inadequacy. You could say that it was warranted, that I should feel that way. That Peter's behaviour was of poor judgement and for the greater part you would be right in coming to that conclusion, but it had led me to look deeper, to form a connection with my own behaviours. Yes, my father had left me. Yes, Peter had called me stupid, yet whilst I knew that neither of these things were my fault, both had left me with equal feelings of self-doubt and feelings of rejection. How could I overcome this problem that had plagued me for over 40 years? I didn't think I could be successful or stand in front of a crowd; if I became overwhelmed or emotionally connected, the tears would start to flow. As part of my story, I desperately wanted to learn to overcome what I saw as a major obstacle. By identifying and acknowledging the real issues that lay beyond the initial confrontation, I was able to move beyond the tears. I now knew the cause and effect.

I am sharing these personal insecurities with you so that we can get to know each other better. Hopefully you will see where this can take you, because the most important thing we need to achieve together through this journey is to align your heart with your head and learn to leave the past in the past. Unfortunately, most of us go through our days stumbling along the bumpy road called life. Some choose to simply give up because it's the least complicated option. Others continue to battle on, no matter how hard it is ploughing through. I know that you are here right now because you are one of those people that never wants to give up. You continue to strive ahead, no matter how hard the going gets, even though it's been hard. It would be nice if life could be a little kinder to you, but regrettably it is the hard knocks in life that have made you who

I am guessing you have also asked yourself many times, why is it harder for me? You know what they say: "Life only challenges those who are strong enough to handle it."

you are today. You probably underestimate your strengths all the time. Focus on being you; start to appreciate who you are and what life's journey has taught you along the way. Think about how you have managed to pick yourself up and travel the hard road day after day. Is it because you want to believe that the toughest part is now done, and you are over the worst? Is this how you motivate yourself to continue? I believe so. So why is it that you continue to do the same thing day in day out, expecting a different result?

I am guessing you have also asked yourself many times, *why is it harder for me?* You know what they say: "Life only challenges those who are strong enough to handle it." You're probably thinking, "Come on, be fair. I've had more than my fair share—give me a break." Knowing all this about yourself has probably been the very thing that has kept you strong, moving forward in the face of adversity, but without the missing pieces, you can't seem to get where you are going—that's where I fit in. Together, we will master the skills necessary to make the changes you need to grow and be the person you truly want to be. After all, you must have had some great skills, talents or behaviours that helped you get here. What skills am I referring to? The ability to say enough is enough; the skill of resilience that has kept you from giving up on yourself, and allowed you to renew your faith in others. The skills that tell you that somehow things will change and the hope that life will get easier. Let me say this; if you read my book, decide that today is the time for change and you fully commit to that road ahead, you cannot fail. I know that's a bold claim to make and I don't take it lightly when I say that success is there for you to embrace.

Money is just one element of life. It keeps you from starving. You will have heard the saying, "Money is the route of all evil." But is it? Maybe it's the person who is controlling the money who continually makes bad choices. It wouldn't matter where you lived, or where you grew up; once you have money, if you then suddenly had to live without it you would be lost. Even if you felt you were happy just relaxing and enjoying peace and tranquillity, you would eventually go in search of something exciting, because dreams are what keep us alive. Unfortunately, it's never enough—the more we have, the more we want. People that have never had money and suddenly inherit it or win it most often lose it. Why is that? I believe it's because they don't have the life skills to manage it. Years ago, I saw a guy on a current affairs program who said that a raffle had ruined his life. He had won a multi-million-dollar property, a fully furnished home, yet he said that it had done him no favours. He couldn't afford to keep it as he was unemployed. True, the upkeep of a home is expensive. Property rates alone can be a struggle, especially with an expensive home, but he was homeless before he won this prize.

Let's put this into perspective for a moment. An option would have been to sell the home, buy himself a more modest place to live, leaving himself with enough surplus funds to not only maintain his home, but live a reasonably good lifestyle as well. He also said that, despite now owning a very expensive house, that he couldn't afford to lend his mother money, which she desperately needed to improve her health, because the bank wouldn't lend him money against the home, which he now owned outright. You need to be able to service or repay a loan, rather than just provide security for the risk to the bank. Maybe I am wrong, but it's his interpretation that overwhelmed him more than anything else; his perception that winning this house would somehow solve all his problems. A different outlook on his money position may have saved the day. It's easy to judge a book by its cover I know that having the ability to look within yourself and solve a problem is no easy feat.

Have you spent your entire life so far wishing it could be different? Take a moment to think back to when you were a child. Did you dress up as a princess or a superhero? Did you believe that the world was your oyster and that you were capable of being anyone or anything you wanted? When we were children we were able to visualise living a wonderful life and it seemed to require little or no planning to achieve. So, what went wrong? You could argue that reality simply set in. We spend years learning skills that most of us will never need or implement, yet weren't taught invaluable life skills. You learn to conform and being a dreamer doesn't cut it anymore.

You hear it all the time: that's life. Life got in the way. You made decisions — or others made them for you.

We have so many limitations imposed on us. Sensibility must form part of the structure and rules need to be applied to create a healthy environment for learning. However, we see these restrictions and apply them liberally throughout our lives. What I'm trying to say is that we focus on things that aren't important and ultimately destroy our dreams. It would be wrong to say that this is the same for everyone. There are always a few that seemingly

skate through life without hurdles, but they are not here now—you are. You're here because you want more than what you have now. To go back to that happy place; the place where dreaming of a wonderful life was possible.

Unfortunately, what went wrong along the way was life. You hear it all the time: *that's life.* Life got in the way. You made decisions—or others made them for you. These are what I refer to as your story; the journey you have travelled so far. It's every sad or heart-breaking event, delicately mixed together with a few wonderful moments or memories that often get neglected or lost along the way. You are here today because you have most likely chosen in the past to focus all your energy holding on to those sad moments that have plagued you throughout your life. Often, we are drawn into the difficult times; without realising, we get caught up in them, preventing us from moving forward. Those dreaded memories that cause us so much hurt and pain incapacitate us. Negativity has so much more power over us than positivity, which fades into the backdrop of life that we find ourselves asking "what if?" Saying things like "if only I had..." which in turn only creates more disorienting power over us. The plan now is to remove yourself from the past and throw your passion into creating a different future. So what is the solution? How do you prevent life getting in the way?

CHAPTER

9

Why Me?

"Why me?" Or worse still, "Why me, again?"

The question that most of us ask ourselves at one time or another is rarely associated with times of happiness or joy. Have you ever known someone to win something and ask, "Why me?" On the contrary, it usually only rears its ugly head when something doesn't go as planned or life throws us a challenge. Have you ever found yourself driving yourself completely crazy asking this question? It's only natural to wonder why disasters or confronting situations happen to you. It's hard to muster up enough energy to fill yourself with the motivation and spirit to keep moving in a forward direction in the face of adversity or tragedy currently afflicting you or your loved ones. Have you ever noticed how some people seemingly float through life, avoiding snags along the way, while you hit so many brick walls it's hard to keep yourself moving. It isn't because you are weaker, less intelligent, or take more or less risks than those who are not afflicted. Unfortunately, this is the most frustrating part. Very few of us will ever discover the secret that holds those answers. I guess if we held the power, none of us would ever be afflicted again. Doesn't that sound lovely.

From situation to situation we move throughout our lives. Some cope and some don't. Is it strength of character or just plain luck? Some may disagree, but I believe it's an invaluable skill set that allows you to survive a negative experience with your life still intact. Some have the willpower to do whatever it takes to go from disaster to success, irrespective of the trauma involved. That doesn't mean that you are without fear. One event is often all it takes to change you. For some, the occurrences continue relentlessly, almost as if they are hounding you down and trying to break you—but can they? Have you allowed yourself to be consumed by trauma? Maybe you aren't sure how to answer that. Please don't get me wrong; it would have been very easy to give up rather than continue. Have you come to the point in your life where you are prepared to drop the "why me?" and break free from it? Let's work together until you can comfortably say that you have overcome the power that question holds over you. Perhaps today was the first time you consciously became aware that you have been feeling this way. This is what I refer to as the victim mentality, whereby you have accepted this

> *Some may disagree, but I believe it's an invaluable skill set that allows you to survive a negative experience with your life still intact.*

as being normal for you. This can present itself in many ways; you may believe that only bad things will happen to you, that you don't deserve good things or that it is your fault that these things keep happening.

For me personally, my quest is to overcome the thought that being a victim is even a small part of who I am. Instead I choose to bravely challenge it head-on. In today's day and age, so much focus goes to nurturing and enhancing one's physical appearance. This can be in the form of massages, pedicures, manicures, spray tans, eyelashes, acrylic finger nails, tattoos—the list goes on. Regrettably, the most important aspect of health is usually forgotten and that is to nurture the mind. But that's not true; you regularly relax with a book, lay on the beach, go on holidays. While relaxation and time out is great, how much time do you invest in understanding and expanding your mind? I am not referring to books but reflecting on your inner self. Thinking is unrated and often neglected. How often do we really sit down and question our attitude towards life? Why our life isn't where we would like it to be and what we should change to make it happen? The definition of insanity is doing the same thing over and over and hoping for a different outcome—are you guilty of that? I prefer to use this saying: "Give a man a fish, he eats for a day; teach a man to fish, he eats for a lifetime." Learning and expanding your mind means to grow, and through personal growth and useful mindset strategies you can make incredible changes in your life, and the lives of those around you. Expanding your mind and thinking differently is also a life skill and legacy you can pass on to your children.

Staying comfortable means staying safe and safe is where we all want to belong. I know you have heard it all before, but that comfort zone you so cosily sit in that you call home is preventing you from allowing the real you to shine through. So why is it that we do this? You may feel that if your true self remains hidden, then if someone hurts you, subconsciously they didn't hurt the *real* you. It's like emotional armour. Putting yourself out there is risky.

10

A journey of self discovery

"What doesn't kill you makes you stronger"

"When you go through hell, your own personal hell, and you have lost – loss of fame, loss of money, loss of career, loss of family, loss of love, loss of your own identity that I experienced in my own life – and you've been able to face the demons that have haunted you... I appreciate everything that I have."

— DAVID CASSIDY

It is Wednesday 8th November 2017. A day of great significance—our 25th wedding anniversary. At 51 years of age I have now spent almost half my days married, and life is better than I could have ever hoped. I have a beautiful and supportive family with three teenagers and a loving husband. Even better still, I have managed to tick off everything on my bucket list and now find myself searching for new places to discover and things to do. Life hasn't always been kind and I say that for an important reason. If you had asked me 26 years ago what it might have looked like, I could certainly never have envisaged the fabulous life I am privileged to have today.

Before sharing this part of my journey, I feel I need to once again emphasise the true focus and purpose for allowing you into my private life. By sharing in my anguish and joy, I hope you will be able to engage more deeply in your own life, learn to forgive yourself and see that anything is possible with a positive mindset and a different perspective or outlook on life. I have continued to strive and reach for better and through adversity I have seen rewards. This is my hope for every one of you. I want to pay attention

I have continued to strive and reach for better and through adversity I have seen rewards. This is my hope for every one of you.

to this because some of you out there are living a life nowhere near your full potential. You are settling for less because, for whatever reason, you either believe you don't deserve better or maybe you think what you have is as good as it gets. Deep down, you know it's not what you really want, yet you are prepared to live a life unfulfilled. When you think differently and your mindset evolves, it allows you to see a different future. If your life isn't everything you dreamed of, it's time to re-evaluate. Easier said than done, I know, but you need to learn to trust your heart. These may be the very words running in circles in your mind, that you have spent so long trying to suppress that you don't even realise you are doing it anymore. On the other hand, it wouldn't surprise me at all if you secretly know you are doing this, because I have been where you are. Trust your heart, listen to your soul and grab onto every moment. We are all here for way too long to be living half a life.

I would love so much for you to join me as I share with you my innermost thoughts and dreams, on what has been my journey of self-discovery. It hasn't always been the way it is now; the majority has been fraught with pain. You have probably heard the term *what doesn't kill you makes you stronger*. Let's face it, it would be great to benefit from the teachings of others rather than have to experience first-hand all the negatives that life can throw our way. My life experiences may not be the same as yours; some have been more than I would ever want to relive. I am a bit of a numbers person. I try not to get caught up in superstition, but you can't fight the numbers, given that they often miraculously fall into place, as they have for us. As we journey together, you will notice that I sometimes refer to a particular numbers, because they have become somewhat symbolic, a kind of lucky charm—at least that's how it feels for me. We all have our quirky ways and this one seems to raise its head every now and then. Growing up, I saw the number three as my lucky number. I was born on the 3rd, as was my brother. My mother was born on the 30th, we lived at number 13—unlucky for some, but not for me—and there were three of us: my mum, my brother and myself. Totally logical so far, right? When I married Frank my new lucky number seemed to be eight. Frank was born on the 5th, three plus five is eight. We got married on the 8th, which was chosen because it was my grandparents' wedding anniversary. They were married for 40 years, so it seemed like a good omen especially given my father's family history with broken marriages, which raised all sorts of superstitions for me as you would know from reading the first part of my story. Our first home after we got married was number eight, the second 48 and the third 78. Only now, years later it lead me to make the connection that we had always unconsciously chosen homes that had included the number eight but once we started to move away from our lucky number eight, things didn't seem to work out as well. A little corny I know, but we all do and think things that give us a sense of happiness and reasoning to help us get through the more challenging times. Trying to somehow find logic when there appears to be none.

Just four years ago in August 2013, life seemed to finally be back on track. Having managed to put most of our money issues behind us, at least to a point where we could breathe a little easier and actually enjoy life again. We had just returned from taking the kids on a mammoth 17-week overseas trip which was initially just Europe, including a visit to Frank's family in Italy. However, I always wanted to see new places, so our trip grew from three months to four and now included a tour of Egypt and Jordan, and a private yacht trip around the Greek Islands. The kids would now gain a knowledge of Egyptian and Greek mythology as well as experiencing life on a yacht. I wish I could say the yacht trip was better than I had expected, but it was quite the disaster after we blocked all four toilets on the yacht! Frankly up until then we had spent far too long grieving for what our life should have or could have looked like had we not made the choices we did. In life we all make choices, some good and some not so good. The true pearls of wisdom come from our ability to lift ourselves up out of the dark and into the light, where you can reflect on what has happened and look to the greener pastures ahead. To learn, benefit and grow from these challenges rather than letting them take you down.

Upon returning home from our wonderful trip away I went into the local bank. The manager approached me and asked if I was still looking for full-time work. I did hesitate for a moment before responding. Although it seemed like a fantastic opportunity, I wasn't totally sure that the timing was right or that it was a route I wanted to take. For a moment I considered whether I should even mention it to Frank but then out of my mouth came the words, "I'll need to discuss it with my husband." A sense of guilt came over me. I felt a little selfish that I wasn't putting the finances of the family before everything else. After holidaying for such a long time it felt so nice having freedom and for a moment, going back to work full-time didn't seem like an attractive proposition, knowing that I'd still have to manage the household—and then there were the kids to consider. The girls would be heading off to high school next year, and for now the primary school was only 150 metres away, so they'd be safe walking to school alone. I know for some

> *Although it seemed like a fantastic opportunity, I wasn't totally sure that the timing was right or that it was a route I wanted to take.*

that may sound really silly or over-protective but considering my plan in life had always been that I would have children and be a stay-at-home mum, this was a time when I had to re-evaluate, stop and assess my priorities.

Would me leaving home before the kids woke up really be something I was comfortable with, especially knowing that they slept like rocks and didn't wake up, even when the smoke alarm was blaring away? On the flip side, it offered security and a regular weekly income, something we hadn't been accustomed to with me having been self-employed for the last ten years. At the time, it seemed like a much harder decision than I could ever have anticipated, but they assured me that as a home finance manager with one of the Big Four banks in Australia I would have some flexibility around working hours, a regular monthly income injection into our not-so-healthy bank balance, and better still, no more waiting for the commission run. I could work with clients for six months or more before getting paid, so I was constantly planning ahead to ensure a regular pay run. This job promised stability—we could finally start planning for a great future. I think that really sealed the deal for me. The bank also told me that they were looking for someone who is passionate about serving the customer and that fitted me like a glove. The interview focused around customer care and it all seemed too perfect. Finally, at 47 years of age, I had found a position where I could be accepted and appreciated as an employee for doing what I do best—putting the customer first. By now you are probably thinking, "I wish I could find that for myself." But was it everything they promised?

Banks, lenders and mortgage brokers are generally all focused on what they do best—making money. Don't misunderstand me; they are just doing want they are supposed to do, nothing more, nothing less. The bank appeared to have their value system aligned perfectly with mine. What I got instead was a huge headache, along with huge sales targets, that focused solely on selling more home loans. I was told, "You don't have time to teach people how to repay their debts or understand their loans—you just need to make more sales." I know they have shareholders to account for, but I have different core values that pushed me in a different direction. My passion is to educate people to understand their money and make the most of it. I had lived 40-plus years creating and living by a money plan and achieved everything financially I had ever set out to do. I wanted to share this knowledge with the world. It may sound corny, but I really do want to make a difference. I feel as though by sharing my passion I am doing what I was put on this earth to do—to somehow make a difference.

My view is simple: yes, customers want to be served but they also need to be cherished and treated as humans.

Not long after I started, a new state manager came in and he changed the way things were done. He had set sales targets for everyone in the branch that crossed over so much that everybody that walked through the door was a moving target. We were told that customers want to be sold to, and while I agree that is true *to a point,* in exchange for the sale they want you to look after them. My view is simple: yes, customers want to be served but they also need to be cherished and treated as humans. As I have already mentioned, I try to always live by the saying *do unto others as you would have done to you.*

Three months in and this job was not what they said it would be. The pessimist in me would love to say, "Is it ever?" But really, it was far from what I wanted. The branch manager was an ex warehouse guy and didn't have a clue what he was doing. He tried to reassure me that things would improve but the constant badgering and degrading questioning—*why aren't you able to sign customers up?*— was downright depressing. I just couldn't seem to find as many customers that qualified for loans as they wanted. The customers that I did see loved my work; there just wasn't enough of them coming through the doors. Despite the customers not qualifying for loans, I was constantly pressured to sign them up, rather than using our time together to focus on building relationships, which I believed would eventuate in loans occurring at the right time for the customer. I never imagined fraud within the banking system. On one occasion, I was told to go and sit with a young twenty-something and watch her as she was hitting all the bank's crazy, unrealistic targets.

After returning to my branch the manager asked me, "So how did it go? Did you learn anything?" I simply replied, "Well if you like fraud it was great!" With a real sense of anger in his voice he said, "That's a big accusation!" and asked why I had said that. I told him that the customer had clearly told her he was married with three children, yet she had entered single with two children. I had sat watching her enter his data, and anticipated the decline message, but what surprised me even more was that she didn't appear to know it would decline before she entered the data, nor did she feel she was doing anything wrong. Was it any wonder she was meeting target and I wasn't? After the customer left, she asked me if I had any questions. "Just one," I replied. "Why did you enter single instead of married, and two children rather than three?" She casually replied, "I didn't want to keep him waiting too long. I was going to go back after he left and update the system." Surely she didn't think I was that gullible. How is it that staff like this are valued, despite their lack of enthusiasm, conscience or even care for the customer, yet here I was willing to give my everything.

Every Friday morning, we would congregate over a group telephone conversation which I felt was demeaning and frankly insulted my intelligence. The team leader would ask, "Belinda's having a bad week, maybe someone would like to share how to get the deals done?" They had already revealed their secrets to me. Not fraudulent as far as the law goes, but certainly fudging the figures within the system. Holding back deals and carrying them over to the next week, pretending they had appointments who mysteriously cancelled at the last minute. I had never worked in such a pathetic environment filled with artificial bullshit flowing like a river. I was not accustomed to this and found it hard to swallow. The manager tried desperately to offer solutions. "You could price match by offering a 0.8% discount!" He had no clue that his offering was in fact less than the offer of 0.9% displayed in the window. The bank was far from a perfect fit for me. I am passionate about making a positive difference in the lives of all my customers and this clearly wasn't working out for me, not to mention the stress it was putting on me both physically and emotionally. The staff were the nicest people I had ever worked with and treated me with respect, but it wasn't enough to keep me there. I don't need to tell you that my banking experience was short-lived.

After three excruciating months, I was finally back to my honest self. The real me wasn't allowed to be in that corporate environment. Returning to the bank that Monday morning took on a whole new perspective. We are a team at home and we have a family to consider, so I had to okay it with Frank. I had to ask him if he would allow me to follow my heart and pursue my true passion, which meant leaving the bank in the dust. He fully supported me, although somewhat reluctantly. At this point, money was still not yet plentiful for us, quite the contrary. We really did need that extra second income, but thankfully he still allowed me to resign from the bank that morning and embark on my newly enhanced and amazing "Find Your Zero" journey.

> *We don't all have the luxury of quitting our jobs, nor do I suggest you do that. This is about finding a balance.*

I guess for some of you reading this, me quitting my job could be frustrating. We don't all have the luxury of quitting our jobs, nor do I suggest you do that. This is about finding a balance. I recommend if you find yourself in this position and you don't have the luxury of quitting, that you start to seek your ideal position whilst still having a regular income. As they say, "Good things come to those who wait."

I wanted to move away from being a mortgage broker and focus on sharing and teaching the skills of effective money management. Over the years I had discovered a common thread between all my customers. Despite earning relatively good incomes most, if not all, were still struggling to make any progress. Some were even struggling to survive telling, me that they were virtually living week to week, not to mention that, despite never defaulting or missing a payment, most now owed more than when I had visited them ten years earlier. My objective is not about getting people out of debt, but rather making the dollar stretch further through my zero concept. It's about showing people where they break even, as many are spending more than what they're bringing home. The ugly truth is, in doing so, you are often fighting within yourself to either keep up appearances, be it consciously or not, and learning to cope with the stresses of everyday life, all the while trying to balance family and work. I understand, we all need a few extra luxuries along the way. However, it's all those little things tallied up that end up costing far more than anticipated, and while you believe you have accounted for all your expenses there just never seems to be anything left over. This is when the important things like a second payment on the mortgage or a well-earned holiday come into play.

These days, the easiest solution is to reach for the credit card and what do you know? There just happens to be an attractive interest free period or a balance transfer at 0%. It all just seems to work out fine in the end—but does it? Are you truly happy with a 30-year mortgage? I assume that for most the obvious answer is yes. This is where I differ. There is no way I want a 30-year plan; to me that seems like infinity and beyond. Personally, I can't follow a plan that stretches beyond a year, two at the most. Nothing in your life, other than the obvious, should span such a long-term plan if you are to maintain momentum.

Having returned from a recent trip to Thailand, I was feeling refreshed. I headed down to the school as I did most days to pick up the kids and, as I was a little early, I decided today was the day. I parked the car outside our old house and proceeded to knock at the door. Amy, the nice English lady that had bought my second-hand uniforms, opened the door and invited me in. As I looked around the home I instantly realised, I actually loved my new home better—who would have thought? Better still, had I not had the courage to face my demons head-on, then I would never have truly appreciated my new home. Suddenly, I was at peace with it all and went home proud as punch to tell Frank what I had discovered that day.

In my constant quest to improve myself I became an education junkie, seeking out and attending courses, continually trying to improve myself. In doing so, I quickly started to join the dots. I have always been a strong advocate for personal growth being the route of everything. My son and I attended a seminar in Sydney. Actually, I booked in Melbourne, then realised it was in Sydney so ended up covering the extra costs of flights and accommodation for both of us. Lesson there—always read the fine print carefully. It was good that it was away from home as it forced him to attend the whole weekend, because he didn't have an escape route. I have always considered myself to be a strong, confident and determined woman and a bit of an extravert, but deep down I am sensitive and compassionate, definitely not one for confrontation. I have always felt that was my biggest flaw. When I feel threatened or get angry, I lose all sense of control and the crying begins. I am only just now learning to understand the triggers and find ways to overcome or avoid the tears; not always successfully, but I'm working on it. First I needed to identify the underlying issues. I have always been truthful and, let's face it, most of us hate to face the truth. I crave self-analysis, even to my own detriment, in an attempt to correct every single flaw. I do this by dissecting my life one piece at time and I am brutally tough on myself in doing so. I am constantly driven to search out and conquer my demons.

Back to the conference. I'm in a crowded room full of wannabe entrepreneurs, all buzzing around selling their products. Meanwhile, I ask myself, "What am I selling?" It wasn't until that exact point in time that I was confronted with truth that I didn't know what I was all about. What was I really trying to achieve? A sweet lady by the name of Jodie stood in front of me, bouncing with excitement and

I had entered the room ready to conquer the world and yet here I was standing like a bumbling fool, speechless and overcome with self-doubt.

said, "Okay, I'm ready! Go ahead, sell me your product!" Totally out of my comfort zone, I broke down. Furious with myself, I stood there completely frozen. Jodie was not at all flustered by my crying and again asked me, "Why don't you know what you're selling?" At this point in the conference I felt as though everyone in the room had a plan except me. I had entered the room ready to conquer the world and yet here I was standing like a bumbling fool, speechless and overcome with self-doubt. The outside world see me as a self-confident, empowered person. While I am all those things, I put such high expectations on myself that I don't understand why I hold back. To be human means we all have personal traits that make us who we are; we wouldn't be human if we were perfect. There is no such thing as being perfect. It would take away the challenge and the drive to be better, which is what keeps me going every day.

Not bothered by my tears, Jodie asked what was wrong. "I don't know," I replied. I wasn't fooling her though. She looked into my eyes and said, "Belinda, you know the truth. I don't believe you don't know what is causing you to feel this way." For a moment, I wondered what she meant. Looking back now, it was the sense of failure in a room filled with people cleverly scouting around selling their products full of excitement that suddenly caused an overwhelming sense of confusion. She prompted me again. "So, are you a mindset person or a money person?" Perplexed, I felt as though I didn't even know the answer. How could it be that I had spent all this money coming to attend a course and I wasn't even clear about my product or what I was offering? To cut a long story

> *She looked into my eyes and said, "Belinda, you know the truth. I don't believe you don't know what is causing you to feel this way."*

short, Jodie turned to me and said, "Belinda you do know what it's all about. It's inside you, you just need to follow your heart."

My mission and vision immediately became clear. That night, as I sat in the hotel room with my son, my head was abuzz with thoughts. Finally, my course structure had the contents it needed to be fabulous and it had all changed so dramatically for the better. If I was really going to help my clients, I had to teach them to dig deep and focus on the real facts: their strengths, weaknesses, fears. So, who are you? And are you being true to yourself, living the life you envisaged for yourself, or have you lapsed into an *it will do* mindset, compromising to survive instead of choosing to thrive?

I came to this conclusion because that's what I had been doing all along. When I could finally accept the truth as it stood before me, my vision became so clear. I had spent my life searching for answers. With these answers always came new and improved plans and with those plans came growth. I had an important message and suddenly I realised I needed to incorporate it into my programs. I now know the reason I missed it for so long was because the truth hurts. Being honest about our disappointments, fears, triggers and insecurities is a huge gamble. It feels like you are exposing your wounds for the world to see, but with it comes enormous personal growth, confidence and a true sense of worth. By entering and dealing with your personal space, you are showing your vulnerability and exposing your innermost fears, but it's also about granting yourself the permission to unleash your full potential. In each and every one of us there is a silent dream and with education comes a sense of power.

From my own perspective, the reason power seemed so bad is that I was always made to feel like it was greed. My desire to want more, or for wanting to achieve, made me feel selfish so it comes back to your perspective. Perception is reality. That's the key to all of this. What you perceive to be true will be true for you. It's about having the confidence to reach outside your comfort zone. Why don't you reach for the stars? Is it for fear of judgement by others? Probably no one is even looking. A fear of failure? You can't fail if you never try. What about a fear of success? There are so many potential reasons.

We all dream of good things happening to us but often, when times get tough, we end up getting caught up in the negative instead of seeing the exit sign to a better life. Before the ugly reality of life sets in and tells us we must comply, think for a moment about the schooling system, which teaches us to behave and comply to rules. Honesty, which I personally find very rewarding and a most valuable attribute is advocated, but only to a certain point right? Then it's a case of keep your opinions to yourself and stop treading on toes. Maybe it even twists around to bite you on the bum where you're seen as a troublemaker.

11

Revelations

"The Voice of Mortality"

"In the end, you're trying to find God. That's the result of not being satisfied. And it doesn't matter how much money, or property, or whatever you've got, unless you're happy in your heart, then that's it. And unfortunately, you can never gain perfect happiness unless you've got that state of consciousness that enables that."

— GEORGE HARRISON

Fast-forward to 31st July 2015 and everything is looking pretty good for me. I admit it took a little longer than I expected, but with little money in the budget to get the business up and running, I couldn't employ extra staff for marketing and design, so I found myself doing everything for the company alone. What I achieved was incredible. I had now documented all my informal courses into workbooks and created workshops. I was starting to get bookings and my customers were happy. I could now show everyone how to reduce their debts significantly. I was helping them to grow and enhance their lives. The next step was marketing. I had finally completed the design work for my latest flyers and that afternoon, 10,000 flyers arrived in a box delivered to my front door. I was so excited, I took them inside and began checking them out. I received a call from one of my clients who had offered to letterbox-drop them around their area and everything was looking great.

Monday came along. I couldn't forget the date because it was my brother's birthday, 3rd August. Today was the day that all my hard work would finally come to fruition and my courses would be seen by the bigger community. Something stopped me in my tracks. *No, Belinda. You won't be able to handle all the calls.* "Of course I can," I told myself. "This is what I have worked so hard to achieve." That gut feeling was so strong, I couldn't possibly go against it. Every part of me was confused, yet I had to acknowledge it and accept that for whatever reason I simply could not proceed at that moment.

It was a cold Melbourne night. Standing in the kitchen that night I couldn't help but ask, "Is anyone else really cold?" As I said it, I threw my right arm up and my left arm across my chest. My heart sank to my stomach as a huge lump popped out from the side of my right breast. My heart began racing as I ran across the room to my daughter. I hoped it was just my imagination and she wouldn't be able to feel it. "I think it's about the size of a grape," I said, desperately trying to downplay the situation. "It's more like a golf ball, mum." How was it that I had missed something like this? How could it grow so big? It must have been quick. I couldn't possibly have missed a lump that size. Panic-stricken, I reached immediately for the phone and called the local doctor trying to secure an appointment that night, but it was about 6pm at night and nothing was available until the next day. I had no choice but to wait patiently until my booking at 2pm. It was difficult but I tried to remain calm. It was probably just a cyst—everything would be fine.

I woke early on Tuesday morning, having tossed and turned all night. I waited until 8am for the surgery to reopen and call in the hope that I could secure an earlier appointment, as waiting until 2pm seemed liked forever. Luckily, my client Sharon worked at the doctors and managed to secure a 10am appointment for me, so I pulled myself together and made my way down there. I had an appointment to see a female doctor, which was a bit more comforting. As she examined me she said, "Don't stress too much— usually if it's painful its nothing to worry about." This was reassuring. All my panicking was in vain; a total waste of time, I convinced myself. Now I could rest again.

As she examined me she said, "Don't stress too much—usually if it's painful its nothing to worry about." This was reassuring.

I couldn't secure an appointment for an ultrasound and mammogram until Thursday, two days away. I would need to travel an hour to Brunswick just to get in faster. Thursday came around and off I went on my own to the appointment. I guess I thought it was just going to be a routine check-up, no big deal. The government sends you for a routine mammogram every year after 50 anyway, so this was just a practice run. Despite feeling very nervous, I never really suspected anything could be wrong. First up was the mammogram, which was rather uneventful, but being left to my own devices, glancing at the image on the screen I could see the lump clearly. I really honestly thought it was a cyst and that it was all taking so long because they were trying to work out what course of action should be taken to get rid of it. Second up was the ultrasound. This time I asked the sonographer what happens next. "Well, if we find something you will probably need to go straight to your doctor," she told me. "If we don't, then the results should be available about 24-48 hours from now." What she said next though took me completely by surprise.

She looked at me so casually. "So are you going back to your doctor now?" Completely confused and taken aback by her casual approach I responded with the obvious. "Should I be?" "It's probably a good idea," she replied. Suddenly, my mind was flooded and my heart was racing at a million miles per hour. I got up off the chair and walked out to the reception desk to collect my images. The receptionist looked up at me and asked me where my doctor was based. "Newport," I replied. "Good," she said. "The results should get there before you."

Totally bewildered, I walked out to my car. I think I was still in complete and utter shock. As I started driving, suddenly I was overcome with confusion. My mind became muddled, maybe due to fear of the unknown or just the overwhelming what-ifs. Had it not been happening to me, I probably couldn't have imagined the thoughts that could run through your head at a time like this, trying desperately to maintain a sense of calm. After all, I hadn't been given the results and all this worry might be for nothing—at least so

I hoped. I found myself struggling to stay focused enough to make the one-hour drive across town as I embarked on what seemed to be an almost endless journey. I ended up making a beeline straight towards the doctors surgery and luckily the traffic behaved well enough for me to make it there safely. Looking back now, I think I must have travelled there on autopilot. During the drive, Frank called me. I tried so hard not to let on that anything was wrong. Once I arrived, the doctor came out to see me and took me into his room. Despite the receptionist's optimism, the results had not yet arrived, so it was back out to the waiting room. Finally the fax arrived with my results and the doctor asked me to come through. I sat down, waiting for the news, bracing myself. He proceeded reading the report out loud to me. I suppose in hindsight he should have taken the time to read it first before seeing me, but perhaps he didn't expect what was to unfold.

Never in my wildest dreams could I have ever imagined that I would be diagnosed with breast cancer. I can distinctly remember thinking this can't be happening.

My heart dropped when I heard the words. *The findings are consistent with a malignant tumour.* Never in my wildest dreams could I have ever imagined that I would be diagnosed with breast cancer. I can distinctly remember thinking *this can't be happening.* A heart attack would have been far more believable; my cholesterol is a little too high and my weight, well, that's too high as well. But this? Never. I immediately burst into tears. The doctor looked at me, confused. "What did I say?" "You said it's malignant." He didn't know where to look. "Wait, I just need to read this again." He continued to re-read the results, I guess hoping he had misread it. Realising it was a reality, he then tried to console me and it just got worse from there. "People with cancer live longer these days, even up to ten years." All I could think of was my beautiful friend Katia who lost her battle with breast cancer. Ever since then I had seen it as a death sentence. The doctor booked me in to see a specialist the following Monday. I left his surgery, tears flowing. *Why me?* I managed to get to the car and called home. I suppose I should have waited until I got home but I was in complete and utter shock. In some ways I was relieved that it was me and not my husband. I knew I could still work from home. I could get through this. I now realise I also delivered the news to my husband in the same horrible way that it was delivered to me. I just blurted it out. "Guess what? I've got breast cancer."

I called my friend Tib in the USA via Skype; we had regular contact and I just needed to talk. Frank isn't one for talking. I needed to vent and had promised to keep her in the loop. Unfortunately, she had recently lost her beloved sister to a brain tumour so for her cancer was too real. We talked, we cried. I think I was more depressed with the idea that life had picked on me again. She was shocked that the doctors could tell me that it was cancer just by looking at the images. She was convinced that they were wrong and began to make me question it too. By the time Monday came around and we went to the specialist appointment, I was almost convinced that they had made a terrible mistake. The specialist quickly knocked this on the head, insisting that cancer can be accurately diagnosed from an image just by looking at its shape. He explained that mine was shell-shaped, with a protrusion at the bottom and a slight point at the top. He went on to explain that they would need to do a biopsy before surgery on Thursday to see what they were up against. I went across to the pathology unit and proceeded to have the biopsy. Thankfully, Frank was with me. I was in so much pain and couldn't think clearly. He asked for them to inject anaesthetic into the site directly via the hollow needle that they had inserted for the biopsy as I was in the most excruciating pain I have ever experienced—and trust me when I say I am used to a lot of pain. The lump itself was painful, so the insertion of a thick needle was unbearable. They explained that only about 1 in every 1000 patients they see—roughly one patient per year—has a painful lump and that the presence of pain usually discounts cancer. Just not in my case. The biopsy revealed a definite presence of cancer, and so I was booked for a lumpectomy.

The surgery went well. The lump was removed with a clear margin and thankfully it hadn't spread to my lymph nodes, which was a huge relief. I am one of the extremely lucky ones. After removal of the tumour they sent it away for assessment to determine what type of cancer it was so that the appropriate treatment plan could be commenced after a short healing period. Mine was diagnosed as a triple negative, which means that it was negative to Oestrogen, Progesterone and HER2—whatever that is. In some respects this is a definite positive, because it means no long-term life medication plan. On the other hand, they still know very little about the causes of triple negative, except that it may be caused by environmental factors such as stress.

Suddenly, I felt as though I had spent the past ten years climbing to the top of a well, finally reaching up and clasping the top. I was free for the first time ever in my life. My hands positioned carefully on the outer edge, I hoist myself up, when out of nowhere a sudden gush of water has come along and thrown me straight back to the bottom of the well. I found myself slowly drowning. No matter how hard I tried, I just couldn't seem to lift myself beyond the grief. Despite all my efforts to remain positive and motivated, I felt myself slipping into a state of despair. Thrust into that horrible, tumultuous spin-cycle, struggling to find answers, all the while trying desperately to avoid that why me question.

> *It is with hand on heart that I make these revelations to you. I watched my dearest friend Katia lose her six-year battle with this very same disease.*

Sharing this part of my story isn't at all about creating a sense of pity. Quite the contrary. Instead, I prefer to see it rather as a moment of enlightenment. To ease a little of the stress of the process, I found enormous relief in sharing my story with my friends and family on Facebook. This in itself was different, but how so? Incredibly, three amazing "spurts of wisdom" as I would come to refer to them, would eventuate from this new experience. Did you notice that I am referring to cancer as an *experience*, rather than a trauma or crisis? By no means do I want to downplay the seriousness of cancer. Unlike many, I am one of the lucky ones and pray that I continue to remain cancer-free.

It is with hand on heart that I make these revelations to you. I watched my dearest friend Katia lose her six-year battle with this very same disease. We had met in 1998, as we each gave birth to our first baby. As you know I gave birth to a beautiful baby boy and Katia gave birth to a girl named Anastasia. Only in August the following year she would reveal to me that she was experiencing severe breast pain. I insisted that she go to the breast clinic, believing maybe, like me, she had mastitis. She told me that they took one look at her breasts and sent her to see an oncologist. Even as she told me this, I never really comprehended the severity. For her the news was not so good—it had already spread. In fact, I think it was already at stage four, news she chose to withhold from me. That I would not discover until her final months.

The cancer was raging throughout her body like a storm. She was the kindest, sweetest, most softly-spoken and polite woman I have ever met. She put up a tremendous fight, refusing to give up trying everything humanly possible to win the race. I never really appreciated just how strong her fight to stay alive for her child would need to be. Maybe it was because she never complained; maybe it was because she refused to believe it would get the better of her. Regardless, it kept her in high spirits and filled her with the determination she needed to keep going. Despite keeping in touch every now and then, she chose to maintain a safe distance from me. I always told her one thing: "If you ever need me for anything, I will be there for you no matter what. All you have to do is say the word and I will be there." Just days before Christmas in 2004, I received the call I never wanted. It was Katia and in her softly spoken voice she said, "Belinda, I need you to come now." I dropped everything and ran to be by her side.

I was now faced with the unenviable task of helping her prepare for her death, wrapping gifts for her daughter, crying with her and helping her put her will together. After only three weeks she called me and I went to her home. I knew it was the end. I watched on as she made the final ambulance trip from her home, her daughter stood by the glass window, yelling her goodbyes. It was heart-wrenching and given that I was a mother with a child of the same age, I couldn't even begin to imagine how soul-destroying it must have been for her, knowing it was time to say goodbye.

For me, cancer has only shown me hope and personal growth. I always saw myself as a strong and positive woman and yet being diagnosed with a disease that had taken the life of a dear friend after a long and painful fight I found myself almost willing to give up even before the fight had even begun. I struggled to understand why. Was it because I always had this gut feeling that my life would be short-lived, so when it finally struck, suddenly it felt like my destiny was coming to fruition? How could it be that a self-motivated person who thrives on motivating others can suddenly be struck down, almost paralysed with fear of death, rather than putting on my boxing gloves and saying *bring it on, I can win this*? I forced myself to try and understand if this was a natural human reaction. Having children certainly means you almost have no right to give up, but it intrigued me as I tried to comprehend my own thoughts and feelings.

Another interesting part, and probably the reason I chose to look at it as an experience rather than a disaster, was that for the very first time in my life I had a voice. Cancer conjures a strong and serious message and scares the absolutely crap out of most of us, but here I was suddenly dealing with the news none of us want to hear, totally out of blue, and everyone I knew wanted to support me. Almost instantly I was surrounded by love, flowers, visits, food for the family, words of encouragement—the list was endless. I couldn't help but wonder why was it that throughout all my darkest, most troubling and difficult times in the past there was no one? I had suffered the loss of a parent but I was deemed lucky because I was so young, that it wouldn't affect me long-term, I suffered ongoing daily ill health causing extreme pain and yet no-one blinked an eye. We lost our life savings and nobody had so much as a kind word. Yet here I was with an abundance of support because I had been diagnosed with cancer.

> *Was it because this was the first time I had chosen to open my private world and let everyone in on my suffering? Maybe it was because cancer is perceived as deadly and people felt sorry for me.*

Was it the voice of mortality? The fact that I used the channels of social media to share my news with friends that empowered me and gave me a voice? Was it because this was the first time I had chosen to open my private world and let everyone in on my suffering? Maybe it was because cancer is perceived as deadly and people felt sorry for me. It was probably a combination of all of the above. I will leave it for you to decide.

Unexpectedly, all these pearls of wisdom were flowing through my mind and the pieces finally began to slot together. The diagnosis was scary and I admit my life flashed before my eyes as I began looking for answers. Of course, "Why me?" played its little part in my life, until my friend Sue cleverly pointed out, "Belinda, you need to stop looking for why and deal with now." These words were inspiring and just what I needed to get back on the horse. I progressed to the next phase and although I had ticked off what I thought were the most important items on my bucket list, that soon came a cropper when I discovered that being around to see my kids turn 18, 21, get engaged, married, and see and hold my beautiful grandchildren were not on the list.

These are the occasions in life that are determined by time, and time alone can control them. They cannot be brought forward to suit you or your situation. Everything I taught now had a new perspective. Whilst I placed a great emphasis on the need to live for today and plan for tomorrow, it now had a new meaning. Most of my customers choose to live for today and think tomorrow will somehow look after itself, but it doesn't work that way—unless you're counting on an inheritance to save you. Then there are some of you putting everything into retirement not knowing if you'll even live to enjoy it. Now my theory was making more sense than ever. I want you to focus on this:

"Live for Today, Plan for Tomorrow."

Planning my treatment, the worst part was yet to come. The doctors informed me that I would lose my hair. I broke in two. *Not my hair.* I realised that I had placed a huge emphasis on my appearance. I knew I was vain, I won't even try to deny it. After ending up broke just months before my 40th birthday I had embarked on a decade of planning my 50th birthday and now I was going to be bald. Next, the doctor explained that I could expect to put on about 10 kilograms from the steroids. I can still remember sitting there at his desk, wiping away the tears, laughing and saying, "Great! So I'm going to be bald *and* fat." Even as I write this, it is still so raw for me and brings tears to my eyes. My hair wasn't just hair; it was a significant part of my identity. It represented everything that I was. I had nurtured and groomed it in preparation for my celebrations the following year and now it was going to be stripped away. I struggled to come to terms with that more than any other part of the process.

> *I can still remember sitting there at his desk, wiping away the tears, laughing and saying, "Great! So I'm going to be bald and fat."*

My oncologist suggested that there was an ice cap procedure that could be done to try and save my precious locks, but with the thick mop of hair that I had it wasn't likely to work. I had no choice but to try it. I had to do whatever I could to save my hair. At the first chemo session, my wonderful friend Polly came with me for support. She helped comb and wet my hair so that they could fit the ice cap onto my head. It took a huge amount of determination and positive thinking to get through those six hours.

The theory was that by running ice water constantly through the cap that the chemo drugs could not go up to my scalp and damage the hair cuticles. It was agonising pain. I almost made it, getting to the last 45 minutes when I could take no more. Polly and the nurses tried to convince me. "You've come this far, you can't give up now!" I scratched and rubbed my arm to cause pain to deflect from my head and finally convinced myself that if there was a person out there that could do this it had to be me, and so I successfully completed the last hour of treatment. Could I do this another four times, I asked myself? Sure, if I could do it once then I could do it over and over again.

A couple of weeks later the choice was made for me—it hadn't worked. My hair was dropping out everywhere as I walked and slept. I had to come to terms with it and decided to make the brave

move to shave my head. My beautiful kids decided to take the day off school and share the experience with me. They stood beside me as the voluntary hairdresser at the hospital took to my head with the clippers. She started with a reverse Mohawk, straight down the centre of my head. First, I cried in shock and horror. Then we couldn't help but laugh. I looked absolutely ridiculous! The task was over and now it was time to try on a wig. No way I was leaving there with a scarf on my head looking like a cancer patient. As time went by, slowly I embraced the headscarf, watching You Tube videos on how to create some classy headgear.

I had proven to myself that I could do anything, and once again my passion and knowledge grew to a whole new level. I pray that this will be the final major challenge that I will need to take on that the only challenges from this day forth will be those that I undertake to help make you see your life in perspective. I hope you have enjoyed and gathered inspiration, motivation and mostly faith in yourself to choose to live a more prosperous and fulfilling life from today. If you have learned from my story please encourage your family, friends and colleagues to also embark on this rewarding journey. My love, fortitude and spirit can be contagious, but I need you to help spread the word!

> *I hope you have enjoyed and gathered inspiration, motivation and mostly faith in yourself to choose to live a more prosperous and fulfilling life from today.*

Here are just some of the most relevant diary notes I posted to
Facebook throughout my chemotherapy journey and onwards.

Belinda Mangani
August 19, 2015 · ⚙ ▾

Thanks to everyone for asking I have my results from the surgery and whilst I
suppose there are aspects of it that are good there are also some not so
good. The good part which is often the easy part to ignore is that the tumour
was removed with a clear margin and it was not detected in my lymph nodes,
the not so good part is that I have been told that chemotherapy and
radiotherapy is unavoidable because the tumour was 3cm and because it
was negative to hormone receptors which means that it is not feed by either
oestrogen or progesterone which would have meant that they could control
the cancer growth by stopping either of these hormones. This news has been
very emotional and stressing as most of you know I love my hair. Not happy
with the thought that its going to be gone at all and whilst many of you think
that the simple answer is "its only hair it will grow back" that is not helping my
thought processes at this point in time. I know that a masectomy would have
been far worse news so I am most grateful that I do not have to endure that
as well. Not sure when it will all be starting as I now have to do a whole lot
more testing before it can start such as full body scanning, CTs and heart
tests prior to chemo

Belinda Mangani
September 2, 2015 · ⚙ ▾

Hi friends thanks again for all your calls flowers and mostly support. Its hard
to believe that tomorrow already marks one month since I found the lump
which changed my life almost instantly. Of course the implications are
endless my children can no longer say breast cancer is not in their family, life
insurance and travel insurance just to name a few. Whilst money isnt
everything its sad that some doctors exploit your vulnerability and almost
take advantage of your stress. Having private health insurance whilst costly
ensures only speed of treatment. Being a specialist in financial hardship I
cannot believe the system. Some say its all free and others like me with
insurance are faced with bills totalling thousands. As for the rest I finally say
an oncologist who explained my tumour and why chemo is not just necessary
but required asap. Looks like next week at this stage.

Now, two years on, people ask me if everything is all good. I should reply with more conviction and send out more optimistic vibes but a part of me still prays it was just a wake-up call. I think a part of me will always retain an element of fear which is probably not such a bad thing. It may be the key to keeping me on my toes and showing me not take my life or my loved ones for granted. Keeping the fear at a safe distance is a measure of control and a sign for me to constantly monitor my own stress levels, to live within my boundaries and most of all, to not be scared to share my skills with as many people as I can.

ABOUT THE AUTHOR

Belinda Mangani is the proud mother of three teenagers: a son and twin daughters. She has been married to her husband for 25 years and everything she does is with her family in mind. Her greatest passion is travel and throughout her lifetime she has had the privilege of fulfilling all her bucket list items around the world even to the point where she is lucky enough to now be researching new places to visit with her family and add to her new bucket list. Finally after a lifetime of dreaming she can successfully tick off that extra item by becoming an Author and travelling the world to share her message as an international speaker.